CW00815728

New Zealand Fly Tying

New Zealand Fly Tying

The ten-thumbed beginner's guide

HUGH McDOWELL

Published by Reed Books a division of Octopus Publishing Group (NZ) Ltd. 39 Rawene Road, Birkenhead, Auckland. Associated companies, branches and representatives throughout the world.

ISBN 0 7900 0021 0

First published 1984
Reprinted 1985, 1988 (twice), 1991

Typesetting by Quickset Platemakers Ltd
Printed by Caritas, Hong kong

CONTENTS

DEDICATION

This book is dedicated

To everyone who has ever stood in a sports shop and stared longingly at a tray of trout flies, hypnotised by the shining hackles, the bright colours and the glittering tinsel, not knowing what to buy or where to start

To everyone who has ever struggled with silk, fur and feather to create a sure-fire killer that's going to "knock 'em dead" next Saturday

To everyone who has ever known the thrill of landing their very first fish

But most especially I'd like to dedicate it to those of you who have yet to experience that never-to-be-forgotten special moment when you land your first trout on a fly you tied yourself

---

ACKNOWLEDGEMENTS

I would like to thank the following people for their assistance in helping me prepare this book: Frank Lord, Jack Bell, Bill Hamill and Geoff Thomas of Rotorua, and Geoff and Margaret Sanderson of Turangi for information on old fly patterns; Steve Wynn of Ngongotaha for the fish hook illustration on p.15; Kelly (Rotorua) Ltd for assistance with fly-tying tools and materials; my many, many friends in the tackle trade throughout New Zealand for their support; and my late wife Sharon, who, in addition to deciphering my handwriting and typing the manuscript, uncomplainingly cleared up my fly-tying bench, removed hooks from socks and was my constant fishing buddy for more years than she would have liked me to mention.

OF COURSE YOU CAN DO IT!

To those who have never tried, tying a fly seems a hopelessly impossible task. "Oh, I wouldn't know where to start – I'd be no good at that sort of thing; it's too fiddly and I'm all thumbs when it comes to something like that" is the normal response. I once had this comment from a plastic surgeon, of all people! Here was a man who regularly performed operations requiring a thousand times more manual dexterity than would ever be required for the most complex of flies, and yet he doubted his ability to tie even the simplest of patterns.

"How ridiculous!" you say, and yet nearly everyone reacts the same way when the subject of learning to tie flies comes up. I'm not sure why; I suppose it must be the fear of the unknown or something. But think about this: few of us arrive in the world with the ability to do more than cry, feed and perform simple bodily functions, but over the next few years most of us acquire an amazing amount of new skills, most of which involve considerably more learning effort than is ever needed for fly tying. Not least of these is the mastery of a completely alien language in both spoken and written form. Can you even remember how young you were when you first did that? The point is, anyone who has learned enough to read this has proved that by now they certainly have the ability to learn to tie a simple New Zealand trout fly!

"Ah," I can hear you say, "but you can't teach an old dog new tricks! I'm too long in the tooth, my eyesight's not what it used to be, my hands are too shaky", etc., etc. Sorry, it's just not true! I ought to know, I've taught fly tying to *hundreds* of people from all walks of life, both men and women, from eight-year-olds to octogenarians. One man had two fingers missing, another had an artificial arm and one elderly woman was so crippled with arthritis she couldn't use a knife and fork. Yet ALL of them became competent fly tyers. Most people I've taught have learned to tie a perfectly satisfactory fly inside the *first hour of tuition.* If they can do it, so can you.

Why Bother Today?

Tying your own flies means different things to different people. For most, perhaps, the biggest attraction is the tremendous saving in cost. After a few days on the river, where rocks, underwater snags, roots and branches of fly-eating trees still take their terrible toll, the replacement of lost flies can be an expensive business, and it takes a brave man indeed to replenish his ravaged fly boxes at the tackle shop and face the bill without blanching, flinching and developing a sinking feeling somewhere deep in the pit of the stomach.

When you tie your own, you can afford to risk casting into all the snag-infested pools and other hazardous places you never dared before without fear, as replacement of any lost flies is going to be measured in cents instead of dollars.

It is really quite easy to learn, the materials don't cost much, and who knows, you may even end up tying flies for the very dealer whose prices prompted you to start tying your own in the first place. Then you can watch *him* blanch, flinch, etc., when *you* present *your* bill!

We've all known the frustration of not being able to replace an unusual and effective pattern which has suffered a broken hook. ("Never heard of it", "Nobody ever asks for it", "We can't stock them all", etc., etc.) Being able to tie your own means no more than simply sitting down at your bench and making up half a dozen when required.

Then again, there's that problem of what to get Cousin Tom, Uncle Dick or Great Aunt Harriet for Christmas when your budget is as low as a limbo dancer going under an outhouse door. A dozen neatly tied flies makes a welcome, practical and inexpensive gift, as does a bright, imaginative single one to use as a hat-band decoration or brooch (you've always wondered about Cousin Tom, haven't you?)

And of course there's the satisfaction of being able to slip yet another batch of freshly dressed flies into your fly box, knowing that each one is properly and firmly constructed and isn't going to come apart while fishing, not to mention the delicious anticipation of the possibilities of your latest "deadly" creation to be field-tested next Saturday.

But, whatever the original motivation, there is *nothing* to compare with that tremendous glow of pride when you land a fish that took your own fly, one you made yourself . . . oh boy! And if it happens two or three times in a row and your much more experienced, but fishless, mate asks if you have "a spare one of those", that's the ultimate compliment and verily your cup runneth over.

There are basically four types of artificial fly: dries, wets, nymphs and lures. Of these four, lures are by far the most popular in New Zealand and, being larger than the others, are probably the easiest to learn to tie. In addition, the construction methods used for these big flies, unlike the others, are completely unique to this country, and so for all these reasons I have chosen to begin with, and devote more space to, the big New Zealand lures.

If you've never tied flies before but are really only interested in fishing perhaps the dry fly or nymph, I still suggest you begin by tying the lures. It will help you become familiar with both the tools and the basic terminology, and believe me, the practice with the whip finisher alone on the bigger flies will stand you in good stead when you attempt the smaller patterns. Besides there are always those Christmas presents, remember? But before we start, take a moment to learn a little about the origin of these big unique creations. The more you know about them the more interesting they – and you – become.

ORIGINS

When trout were introduced to New Zealand towards the end of the last century, they thrived and multiplied at an unprecedented rate. The cold, clear, unpolluted waters, abundance of food and lack of predators provided an ideal environment, and soon the early sportsmen were catching salmon-sized trout using the salmon flies they had brought from the old country. Now these salmon flies were miniature works of art. Tinsels, furs and silks of every conceivable hue were skilfully blended with intricate arrangements of brilliant feather fragments from some of the world's rarest and most exotic birds, necessitating sometimes as many as 24 separate ingredients for a single pattern. The results were very gaudy confections indeed.

It is thought that early fishing experts believed salmon were attracted to butterflies. Whether or not this is true, I don't know, but there is little doubt that the salmon flies of the day probably bore more of a resemblance to some gorgeous tropical butterfly than anything else a migrating salmon was likely to encounter in fresh water. Needless to say, the creation of one of these complicated masterpieces required the attention of a highly skilled artisan, and the finished article, like all labour-intensive handmade products, was expensive.

But no flies, no matter how well made, last forever. They get cracked off with badly-timed casts, hooked up in bankside vegetation and underwater snags or carried away by particularly boisterous fish. Moths and other insects attack and destroy the feathers, hooks rust and break and, in addition, the twisted loops of silkworm gut that formed the eyes of those early flies rotted and perished in time. So, for a variety of reasons, replacement flies were regularly required.

In England this was no great problem. Since salmon fishing was the privilege of only the very wealthy upper classes, the high price of new flies wasn't terribly important, and the exotic plumage used in their construction was abundantly available from the British colonies in Africa, India and the Orient. However, in New Zealand it was a different story. Here in a virtually classless society, anybody could fish for the big, hard-fighting, silver trout. But import costs made the already costly flies they required an even more expensive proposition. Continuity of supply, too, was something of a problem, while those few enthusiasts with the ability to tie the complicated things themselves often found the necessary materials difficult, if not impossible, to obtain.

Pioneers, of necessity, must improvise, and the early Kiwis were no exception. Soon imaginative sportsmen were creating their own flies from materials that *were* readily available, and from these early efforts evolved a whole new range of flies. These initial efforts lacked the psychedelic brilliance of their butterfly-like predecessors, tending rather to represent forage fish, freshwater koura (crayfish) and other food items more commonly found on the antipodean trout's menu. But they were cheaper, much simpler to tie, more readily available and, most important, they caught fish.

From those early beginnings, the big all-New Zealand flies progressed in leaps and bounds. Inevitably some patterns fell out of favour and vanished, while new ones appeared regularly to take their places. Many others mutated and evolved over the years, due to the whim of the individual dresser, the scarcity of one ingredient and its substitution by another or the advent of an entirely new material. Bodies of mohair and seal's fur have for the most part been replaced by chenille for example; while the once indispensable jungle cock cheeks and golden pheasant topping are rarely seen at all nowadays.

But in addition to component and cosmetic changes, there emerged revolutionary new ideas on fly *design and construction*, some of which *still* endure and indeed form the basis of most of the big New Zealand flies today. It is the distinctly different structural system of these flies that separates them from all other types and makes them completely unique to New Zealand.

Of course, like all good ideas, they've been adopted and copied the world over. I saw my first Red Setter in a Californian steelhead fisherman's fly box, and some years ago another American fishing friend sent me instructions on how to tie a "new fly" he'd used with great success in Montana and which turned out to be nothing more than the ubiquitous N.Z. Orange Rabbit. A Boer (I'm not sure if I've spelled that properly!) recently showed me a Kilwell No. 1 which he had "just invented"; I saw the same fly illustrated in a colour plate of South African fly patterns under the title of "Walker's Killer" in which it is alleged to have been created in 1962. But imitation is the sincerest form of flattery and it is rewarding to know that the Kiwi designs have earned for themselves a permanent place in the history of fly tying.

TYING THE BIG NEW ZEALAND LURES

When first confronted with the dazzling array of big New Zealand flies displayed in a well-stocked sports shop today, the novice may well be filled with dismay. The prospect of learning to tie all of the myriad of different patterns would appear to represent years of intensive study, yet nothing could be further from the truth.

If you look closely you will find most of them are simply cosmetic variations of four distinct construction designs. Master each of these four different designs and you'll find that you can tie almost any lure you'll ever need, merely by using different ingredients. It's that simple.

As far as I know there have never been official names given to all of these four techniques, so for ease of identification I will call them:

Hackle-style
Matuku-style
Pukeko-style
Killer-style

Now I know some of you more knowledgeable readers are going to start quoting patterns that don't fall into the above-mentioned categories. Yes, there are a few, and you'll find instructions for tying some of them listed further on in the book. I've done this because I wanted to emphasise styles of tying that evolved within, and are unique to, New Zealand. Take the ever-popular Hairy Dog, for example. Although widely used today it didn't originate here at all, and you'll find flies of this type have been tied in Scotland, Ireland and England for centuries.

Another factor which may cause some controversy is the listing of alternative colour choices for some part of a given pattern. I have earnestly tried to describe each pattern as accurately as possible, but there are many areas where even the experts differ. I have yet to determine whether a Parson's Glory should have red or orange tail whisks to be technically true to pattern, for example, so I list both. As far as the fish are concerned it doesn't seem to matter one way or the other, and in fact when tying my own Parson's I usually leave the tails out altogether without any noticeable difference in results. But I'm digressing.

Let us first examine the tools we're going to use.

THE TOOLS OF THE TRADE

One of the best fly-dressers I ever had the pleasure of watching was Michael Rogan of Ballyshannon in Ireland. With the hook held between finger and thumb he created the most beautifully tied flies while discussing fishing conditions with me over the counter of his little tackle shop and, as I recall, the only tools he used were a razor blade and a darning needle.

Unlike you and me, Michael was born with only two thumbs against our ten, but fortunately for us there are a number of simple, ingenious and relatively inexpensive devices on the market to help compensate for our deformity, and we should familiarise ourselves with them. A word of advice: As with so many things, the cheapest usually turns out to be the dearest in the long run, so buy the very best tools you can afford at the beginning; they will last you a lifetime and will never let you down. Kelly's of Rotorua market an excellent "Professional Fly-Tying Tool Kit" under the "Kilwell" brand. (I know it is excellent because I put it together!) Every tool in it has a lifetime guarantee — if it fails, they replace it. The English firm of Veniards also produces some excellent tools as do a variety of American manufacturers. But whatever brand you choose, buy the best. You will never regret it.

THE VICE The fly tyer's vice is simply an instrument which clamps on the edge of the table or workbench and serves to grip the hook firmly by the bend with the shank protruding horizontally from the jaws in front of you, so both your hands are kept free.

If you plan to use the dining-room table as a workbench, it will probably pay you to glue a piece of thin rubber (from an old inner tube perhaps) to each of the vice's clamp faces before you begin. This will help prevent marring the table surface and ensure a secure grip .

THE BOBBIN HOLDER During the construction of a fly you will be constantly winding different materials on to the shank of the hook and securing them with a binding of thread. Fly-tying thread usually comes on a plastic spool, and the bobbin holder is a handy gadget which enables you to hold this bobbin (or spool) in your hand and pay out thread as you wind. It consists of a simple frame with a polished tube. The spool is held under adjustable tension within the frame, and the thread runs off the spool and up the tube between your finger and thumb while being wound onto the hook shank.

The combined weight of the bobbin holder and its spool of thread when left dangling is enough to hold the materials fast and prevent unravelling while you answer the telephone, light a cigarette or search for the next piece of material required.

Once again, quality pays off. Cheap bobbin holders often aren't smooth and highly polished at the end of the tube, and the resulting friction frays through the thread, always, seemingly, at a critical moment, and the whole fly springs apart like a jack-in-the-box.

HACKLE PLIERS A good pair of hackle pliers can be a godsend, particularly when using smaller feathers. You will be learning later on that in some flies a feather is secured by the thick end of the stem to the hook shank and the entire feather wound round and round the shank until the tip of the feather is reached. Trying to hold a small feather tip in the finger and thumb can be a frustrating experience, particularly when you get near the end of the winding process and you're "running out of feather". Hackle pliers grip these fine slippery tips firmly for you, enabling you to use almost all the feather, even in the smallest sizes.

The gripping qualities of most models can be improved greatly by gluing a small piece of rubber to the inside face of one of the jaws (manufacturers take note). To operate your pliers simply squeeze to open, place tip of feather between jaws and release pressure, causing the jaws to clamp down and hold the tip securely.

SCISSORS You *can* get away with using a razor blade, but the joy of being able to reach into a forest of material and snip off a rogue hackle or fibre with the point of a good pair of scissors can be compared only to the satisfaction of dislodging a strand of roast beef or a particle of nut from between your teeth with a toothpick after half an hour of probing with your tongue.

The ideal fly-dresser's scissors are small with fine sharp points and were probably originally designed for surgical work. They won't be cheap, but they will cut effectively right down to the very end of the points and will last for years. Don't under any circumstances be talked into buying the kind you find for under a dollar in first-aid kits or embroidery shops, and don't use yours for anything other than fly tying, or lend them. ("I only want to cut out this coupon, piece of string", etc.)

Good scissors are available with both straight and curved blades. I've used both and don't really find one better or more useful than the other.

THE WHIP FINISHER A fly is usually tied by commencing at the tail and finishing at the head. The whip finisher is a handy little tool that will help you finish off your fly with a neat whipping in the very confined space remaining between the material and the eye of the hook.

It is a very controversial tool; many professional tyers don't use it, preferring to whip finish by using their fingers only, but I have never known

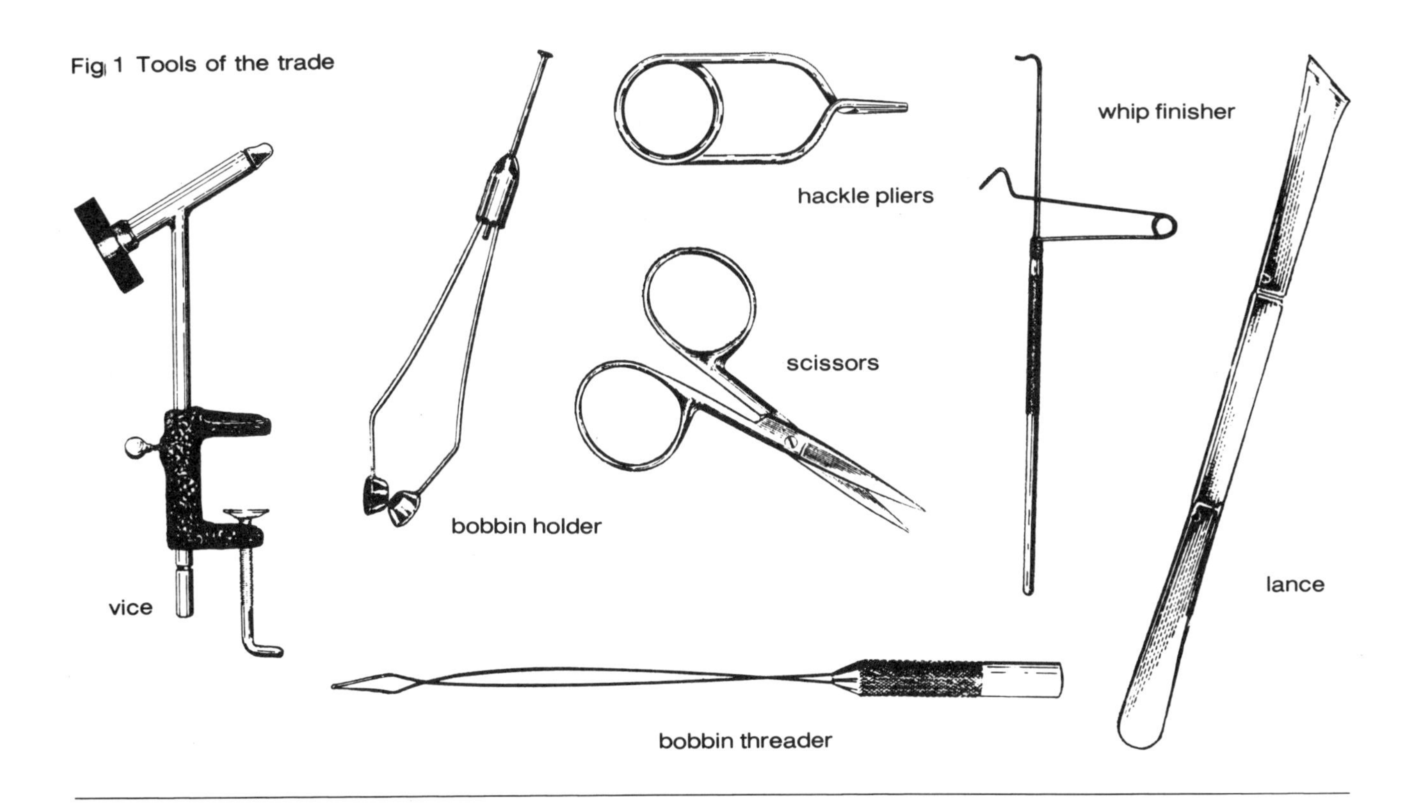

Fig 1 Tools of the trade

anyone to go back to the manual procedure after getting used to the whip finisher.

MISCELLANEOUS A simple **darning needle** is useful for picking out inadvertently trapped feather fibres or unblocking varnish-clogged eyes of hooks. Unfortunately, needles have a habit of vanishing into thin air (at least mine seem to) and a **bodkin** is a practical acquisition. The Kilwell model FT 118 is a particularly ingenious device which features a small, slim metal tube with a needle bonded to one end and a **bobbin threader** attached to the other, thus making its possession doubly desirable.

A fly tyer's **lance** comes in handy for cutting rabbit pelts into the clean, thin strips required for tying flies of that name. You *can* substitute a razor blade, but the double-edged ones can be hazardous to use, and the old fashioned single-edged variety is difficult to find nowadays.

I also keep a supply of ordinary **toothpicks** handy; inserting one in the eye of a newly tied fly prevents clogging when applying protective cement to the whip-finished head.

So having familiarised ourselves with the tools we're going to use, let's now have a look at some of the materials we'll be working with.

MATERIALS

HOOKS

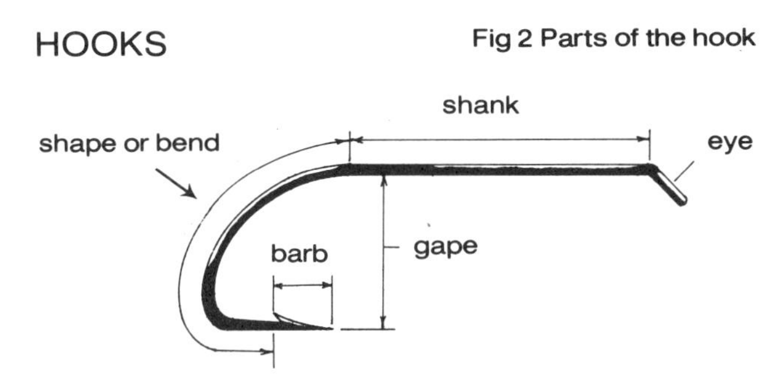

Fig 2 Parts of the hook

The first thing you're going to need is a supply of hooks, and almost any good-quality fly hooks from size 2 down to size 8 will do, so long as they don't have kirbed or offset points – which, I feel, can upset the balance and action of the finished fly. I say "good-quality" because of all the snares and pitfalls in fly tying, poor-quality so-called "bargain basement" hooks would have to be the worst. They are often improperly tempered and so bend or break under stress, the eyes are frequently roughly finished and not properly closed, causing the leader to fray or slip out altogether, and they all tend to rust easily. So why take the time to tie a really nice fly on a hook that is suspect? Take it from me, cheap and nasty hooks belong with bulging cans of meat, remains of old prescriptions, last week's oysters or the year-before-last's nylon – in the garbage can!

The single most popular hook used for tying the big New Zealand lures is unquestionably the Mustad 3666 (fig. 3a), and I suggest the beginner try these to begin with.

Fig 3 Fly hooks

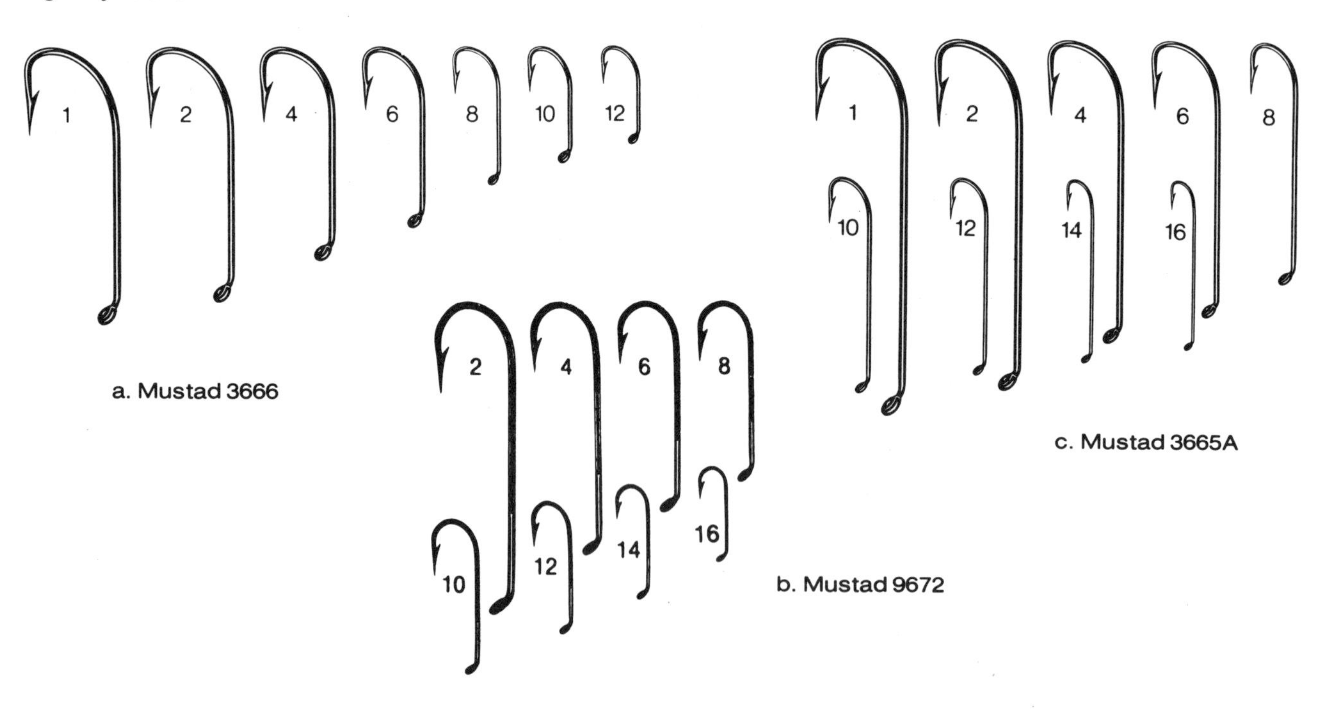

Later, when you progress to more specialised patterns like Matuku Muddlers or super-long, slinky smelt designs, the extra-long-shanked Mustad 9672 (fig. 3b) or even longer-shanked 3665A (fig. 3c) can be useful in helping produce a big fly with a smaller hook-size than would be the case if you tried to tie them with the regular-sized 3666.

Hooks are usually sold in boxes of 100 or in packets of 10. The cost per hook is of course greater when you buy them in packets due to increased packaging costs but, if you are on a limited budget and want to experiment with different sizes and shapes, the smaller quantities are more practical in terms of providing a wide range for a limited outlay.

COCK HACKLE FEATHERS

These are the long, tapered feathers from the back of a domestic rooster's neck or rump. Sadly there aren't as many of the old poultry breeds around today, the Wyandottes, Plymouth Barred Rock, Light Sussex, Buff Orpington, Leghorns and Rhode Island Reds of yesteryear having all but vanished, probably due to hybridisation for the modern "battery broilers".

Fortunately for the fly tyer, science hasn't yet managed to create a chicken that grows up prepacked in cellophane, and many useful feathers are still widely available. You can buy them in packets of a few dozen or (better value) as "capes", "half capes" or "necks" (i.e., still attached to a swatch of the original owner's skin!), or you might even be able to scrounge some next time a farmer friend kills a suitably plumaged bird for the pot.

The following is a list of the most likely hackles you'll come across:

GRIZZLE Alternating V-shaped bands of black and white.

HONEY GRIZZLE Alternating V-shaped bands of light and dark ginger.

CREE A grizzle with ginger undertones.

FURNACE A rich, deep reddish-ginger with a black stripe up the centre.

BADGER Creamy white with a black stripe up the centre.

GINGER Ranges from pale buff to deep ginger.

NATURAL RED Ranges from light to dark reddish ginger.

NATURAL BROWN Ranges from light to dark chestnut.

VARIANTS This is a name given to cover the infinite variations of the above. For example, you may find a pale feather shading from cream through buff to dark ginger with a thin black stripe beginning halfway up. It's not a true badger, and it's not a furnace; it's a variant. If you ever see a particularly interesting one that you like the look of, *buy it*. You may never see that particular combination again in your lifetime.

WHITE Probably the most common and least-used of all feathers, yet I've had some good catches on flies using white hackle (see Disco Doll, Grey Ghost).

BLACK Very rarely found in natural feathers, strangely enough (see DYED HACKLES).

DYED HACKLES Usually available in red, orange, yellow, olive, green, grey, magenta, blue and black. Few are completely colour-fast, and some colours may "bleed" on to adjacent materials when the fly is wet, so be warned. You can of course dye your own using white, cream or other pale feathers, but that is another subject altogether.

OTHER USEFUL FEATHERS

PUKEKO Get a friend to bring you a pukeko from his next duck-shooting expedition. The skin will provide thousands of feathers. You can buy both black and blue pukeko substitute (dyed mallard flank feathers), but it's illegal to buy or sell the real thing. Used mainly for night flies.

HAMILL'S PLUMAGE Originally this was partridge dyed a peculiar shade of green. Since partridge seems in short supply, dyed mallard flank feathers are mostly substituted today and work just as well for Hamill's Killer.

COCK PHEASANT RUMP Both the greenish rump feathers and the chocolate-and-cream "church-window" feathers are used in the ever popular Mrs Simpson pattern today.

GREY MALLARD FLANK These are greyish-white with a black fleck. Used mainly for Mallard patterns.

HAIRS AND FURS

SQUIRREL TAILS Red, grey and black are all used for a great number of popular patterns. Goat hair and the new synthetic FisHair make acceptable substitutes.

RABBIT SKINS Essential for the ever popular Rabbit flies. Cut in thin strips *lengthwise*, i.e., in the direction the hair lies naturally, with a safety razor blade or very sharp instrument. Kilwell market an inexpensive lance (Reference FT 119) especially for the job.

CAT SKINS Next time you're shooting and dump a feral cat, keep the skin. If you don't shoot, maybe you have a friend who does; or you can always bribe a possum trapper. Aside from the benefit to both song and game birds, you can make some wonderful "Rabbits" with feral cat skins, especially tawny and black ones.

TINSELS

Tinsel is made in three types, flat, oval and embossed, each type being available in three sizes, fine, medium and wide. In addition, the flat variety also comes in a non-tarnishing material called Mylar, and all of them are produced in both gold and silver. Quite a selection, but all you need for any of the flies in this section are medium oval tinsel and flat wide Mylar, both in silver and gold. If you're on a really tight budget, you can drop the gold!

TYING THREAD

Almost any thread can be pressed into service for tying flies. Personally I use a brand called Monocord which is available everywhere and comes spooled on plastic bobbins which fit most popular bobbin holders. It's very fine and exceptionally strong for its diameter. Although available in a wide variety of hues the colour isn't really important, but black is the most popular.

CHENILLE

This is probably the most widely used body material for the big N.Z. lures. It comes in many colours with red, orange, green, yellow and black being favourites, but other popular shades include white, brown, olive and sparkle, as well as fluorescent pink and lime. Since it's reasonably cheap most of us can afford to buy all of them, but if you really want to keep expenses to an absolute minimum, the first five mentioned will suffice.

HEAD CEMENT

This quick-drying lacquer comes in black and red and is used to provide a protective seal over the neatly whip-finished head of your newly tied fly. A clear version under the title "Body Cement" can also be used for cementing fly bodies firmly to the hook shank. Kilwell market all three in bottles with handy little applicator brushes inside the lids (like nail varnish manufacturers); otherwise you will have to apply with a needle or toothpick.

Incidentally, you can actually *use* nail varnish at a pinch, but it's not as durable and costs about twice as much!

Of course you don't need *all* these materials initially. You'll gradually build up a stock as circumstances (and your budget) will allow.

I suggest you begin with some honey grizzle and some black hackles, a black squirrel tail, a selection of chenille in red, orange, yellow, green and black, a spool each of medium oval tinsel and flat wide Mylar, either silver or gold, a spool of Monocord, some Mustad 3666 Limerick hooks, size 4 or 6, and a bottle of black head cement. With these, using the tools recommended earlier, you will be able to tie dozens of the most popular flies in use today. And don't be afraid to substitute! If the pattern you are attempting calls for honey grizzle which you can't get, use a ginger, cree or a pale furnace instead, because regardless of the colour of the feather, the technique of construction remains the same, and that's what is really important to begin with. If the finished product isn't exactly true to pattern, so what? Few trout read angling books, and I bet they'll never notice the difference!

GETTING READY

I can see it now. The evening meal is over and the dishes washed and stacked away. The children have brushed their teeth and gone to bed, the cat's asleep on the hearth and Mum's watching telly (or maybe Dad is – these days fly tying is certainly not a male-only activity). On the table in front of you lie your fly tying tools and materials, while on the floor beside your chair sits an empty cardboard carton for waste materials. You're ready to start.

Before going any further, I should explain that I have assumed you to be right-handed. If in fact you aren't, I'm sure you can interpret my instructions accordingly. OK, let's go.

(a) Attach the vice to the edge of the table,

adjust the height and lock in position, with the jaws pointing to your right.

(b) Insert a hook in the vice, making sure the point and barb are held inside the jaws with the shank uppermost and protruding horizontally to your right. Clamp jaws up tight — and I *mean* tight.

(c) Check that the hook is solidly secured by applying up and down finger pressure on the shank at the eye, and if the whole hook moves, tighten the vice jaws even more. If the hook bends,it's under-tempered; if it breaks, it's over-tempered. Either way, replace it and go back to (b).

(d) Insert a spool of Monocord between the arms of the bobbin holder and pull off some thread. Take the bobbin threader (that's the funny-looking thing that came with the bobbin holder) and poke the wire loop down the tube from the other end, slip the thread through and pull it back up. (If you didn't get a bobbin threader with your bobbin holder and can't get the tube threaded, use a loop of monofilament.)

(e) Check the arm tension of the bobbin holder by pulling thread from the top of the tube. The spool should yield thread easily, but not so freely as to unwind when the bobbin holder is dangling from the end of the thread. This is important. To adjust, simply bend the arms in or gently pull apart until the required tension is achieved.

HACKLE-STYLE FLIES

Of the four basic methods used in tying the big New Zealand flies the Hackle style is probably the easiest to learn.There are eight standard patterns which all share the same construction technique, so when you can tie one, you can tie them all.

Take the Fuzzy-Wuzzies, for example. There are five of them, differing only in whether you use orange, red, yellow, green or black chenille for the bodies. An Orange Fuzzy-Wuzzy becomes a Red Setter when you switch from black hackles to ginger ones, while Dappled Dogs are merely Fuzzy-Wuzzies tied with fluorescent orange or lime chenille, grizzle hackles and grey squirrel tails. Maybe I should have called the whole series Fuzzy-Wuzzies instead of Hackles, but you see what I mean?

You don't have to limit yourself to these eight either. Let your imagination run wild and experiment with your own combination of hackle, tail and body colours. As you become more adept, you might even like to try tying in two feathers instead of one at each hackle section, using contrasting or blended colours – red and orange, yellow and grey or blue and green perhaps? The possibilities are endless.

I have produced some interesting hybrids this way (see Disco Doll and Rotodyeran Special). A few were successful fish-catchers and many were not, but regardless of whether you come up with a deadly new pattern or a handful of cap decorations, the tying practice will be invaluable and will provide you with a great deal of

Fig 4 How to tie a Hackle-style fly

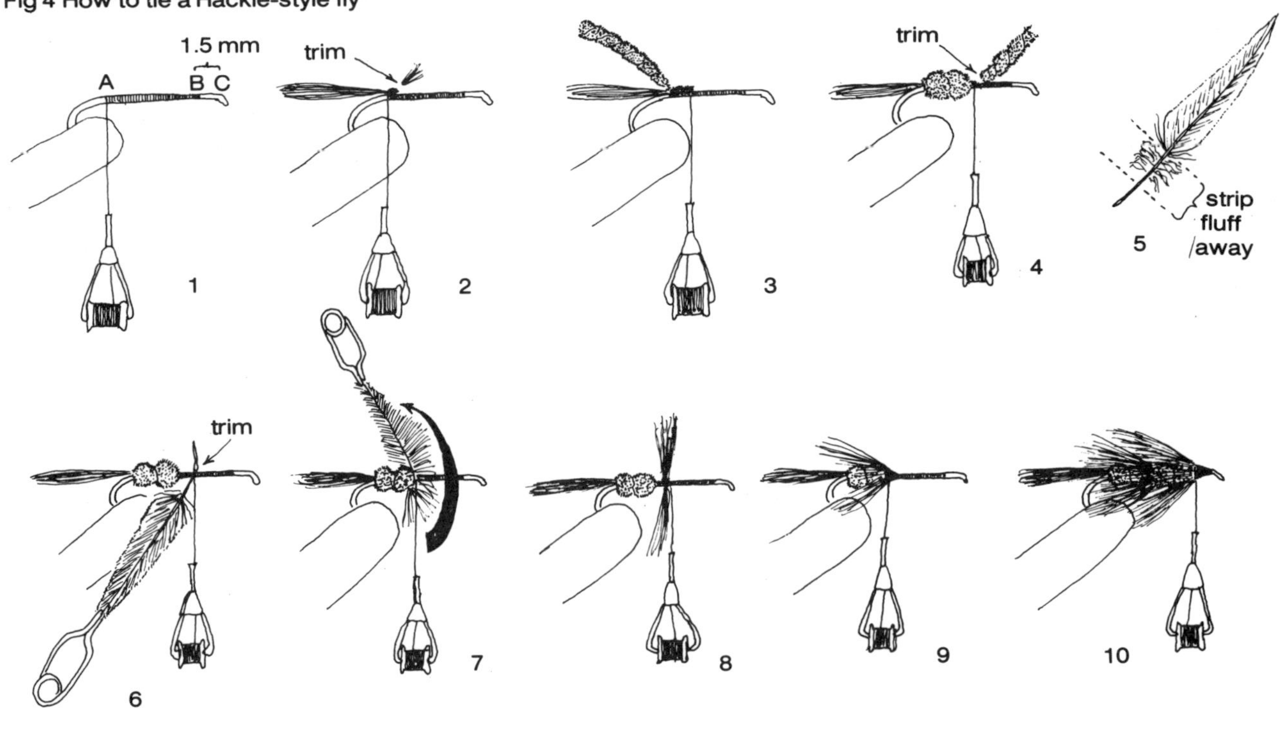

enjoyment and self-satisfaction into the bargain.

One of the keys to successfully producing good, well-shaped Hackle flies is to ensure that both sets of hackle fibres slope back at 45° or more, enshrouding each body section in an evenly distributed conical veil.

HOW TO TIE A HACKLE-STYLE FLY

1. Bind the hook-shank with thread from B to A with a series of firm, closely-wound turns.

   If you've never used a bobbin holder before and are having trouble, here's what you do. Lay it across the palm of your right hand at about 45° (so that the tube crosses the top joint of your index finger), and then close your hand over the bobbin. With your left hand pull out about 5 cm (2 in) of thread from the tube, pinch it lightly to the hook-shank at B and hold it there until it gets trapped under the turns as you wind down the shank, working up and away

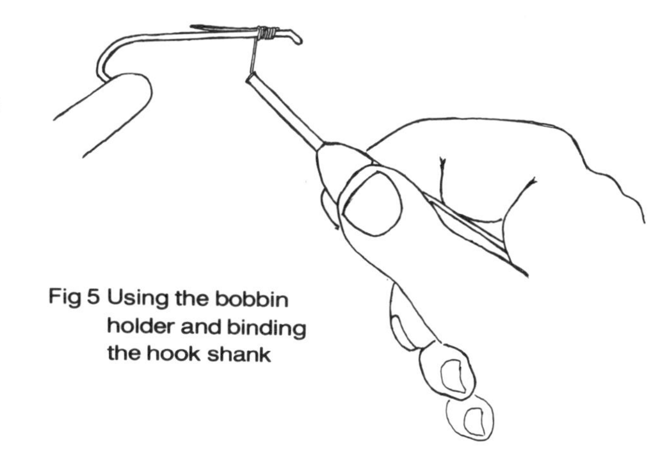

Fig 5 Using the bobbin holder and binding the hook shank

over the top with your right hand (i.e., clockwise looking down from the eye towards the point – see fig. 5). Stop at A and let bobbin holder dangle on about 7.5 cm (3 in) of thread.

The purpose of this binding is to provide a good non-slip base on which to securely bed both the tail and body, *and it is the first step in tying every fly shown in this book.*

2. Next, the tail. Grip a small pinch of squirrel hairs tightly between your left finger and thumb and clip it free from the base of the tail. (The correct amount is probably about one half what you think you'll need.) You'll find a lot of short fluffy fur trapped in round the base of the hairs, so keeping a firm grip with your left finger and thumb pull it away with your right. Hold the bunch of hairs firmly down on top of the shank at about A, keeping your left finger and thumb pressing tightly together. Pick up the bobbin holder with your right hand and bring the thread up, force it back between your tightly-pressed left finger and thumb (don't relax the pressure) and out again over the far side of the shank. Now when you pull down on it, the hidden loop thus formed between your left finger and thumb will in turn pull down on the hairs to hold them securely on top of the shank while the lateral pressure of the finger and thumb prevents them from splaying out round the sides. Repeat the process 4 or 5 times before relaxing your grip, when the weight of the dangling bobbin holder will be enough to keep everything in place (see fig. 6). The result should be a tail bound firmly by the butts on top of the shank at A and protruding back beyond the bend about the same length as A–B. If it isn't, grip it in your left hand, unwind the thread with your right and start over. No, you can't just cut it if it's too long or pull it if too short, believe me! When satisfied, trim off any surplus material to the right of A with your scissors.
3. To start the body take a piece of chenille of about 7.5 cm (3 in) in your left hand and bind one end securely to the shank at A with 4 or 5 turns of thread. Then continue to wind the thread up the shank to somewhere just short of midway and let the bobbin holder dangle.
4. Transfer the chenille to your right hand and wind it up the shank in closely lapping turns, making sure the work on the base of the tail gets buried in the process. Three or four turns

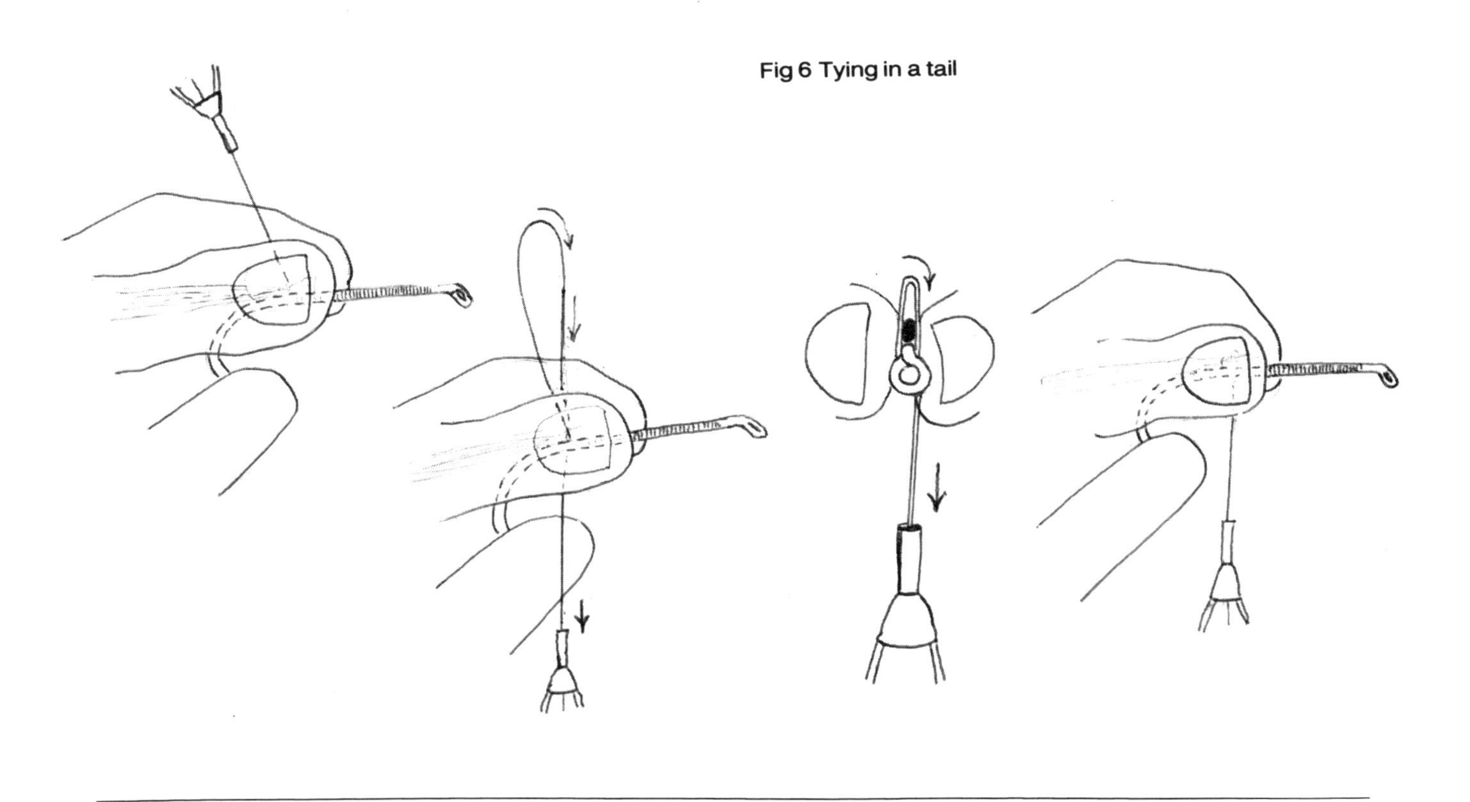

Fig 6 Tying in a tail

should take you to the thread. If it doesn't, wind the thread back to the chenille. Bind down the chenille under 3 or 4 turns of thread. Let the bobbin holder hold it in place while you trim off the surplus. Now wind thread about 3 mm ($\frac{1}{8}$ in) further up the shank, and let the bobbin holder hang there. *This 3 mm is important.*

5. Take a hackle feather in your left hand and with your right finger and thumb remove all the fluffy downy stuff from the base of the central stem. If you look closely at what remains, you will find that the feather curves slightly and that the concave side is quite matt, while the convex side has a glossy surface.
6. With the end of the feather pointing towards the left, the glossy side towards you and the concave matt side next to the hook, bind the stem to the shank at that point 3 mm from the chenille with 3 or 4 turns of thread and clip off the surplus stem. Leave bobbin holder dangling.
7. Take the hackle pliers, squeeze to open the jaws and let them close over the tip of the feather about 6 mm ($\frac{1}{4}$ in) from its end. Bring the feather forward through 180° to crease the stem where it is bound down, bring it back to vertical and, using the pliers to keep it taut, wind over and away from you round the shank, up and over, up and over in the same place until you "run out of feather". Secure the tip of the feather to the shank with 3 or 4 turns of thread before clipping it free. Now leave all secured by the weight of the hanging bobbin holder and examine the work so far.
8. What you should have at this stage is a ring of hackle fibres standing at 90° all round the hook shank about 3 mm up from the end of the chenille.
9. With the fingers of your left hand try and hold all these hackle fibres back parallel to the body while with your right you wind the thread *back* over them for that 3 mm until you reach the

chenille so that they are held sweeping back at 45° or more over the body when you release your grip.

10. Repeat everything from step (3) to step (9), but try to finish the process at B, leaving the space between B and C free in which to do your whip-finished head. Chances are you will have encroached a bit on this area. This isn't all that critical, but you *must* have *at least* 1.5 mm ($\frac{1}{16}$ in) of bare hook shank between the end of the body and the eye, and 3 mm ($\frac{1}{8}$ in) is better still.

There is a detailed step-by-step description of how to carry out a neat whip finish on pages 30–33 (figs. 7 & 8). However, this will take some considerable practice to master, so in the meantime I suggest you finish your fly by winding the thread until you have formed a nice conical head behind the eye of the hook and then tie half a dozen half-hitches or even granny knots to keep it from unravelling after you cut the thread. Now coat the thread thoroughly with head cement, making sure you don't get it on the hackles or clog the eye in the process, and hang it up to dry for 10 minutes.

I recommend that you try to perfect your techniques by tying perhaps 10 or 12 Hackle flies before moving on to the other types, however strong the temptation to do otherwise may be, since so many of the steps you are learning are universal. For this reason I will constantly refer back to Hackle fly instructions in the subsequent lessons, so do make sure you have grasped these fundamentals before proceeding.

Some dos and don'ts in tying a model Hackle fly:
DON'T make the tail too long – the same length as the body is about right.
DO make sure the tail is secured on *top* of the hook shank. If you are having trouble with this, try using a smaller pinch of squirrel hair and re-read step (2).

DON'T leave "gaps" in your work. Try to conceal each binding or tying-in process with the material used in the following stage. For example, the thread securing the tail should subsequently be buried under the first turns of chenille; the thread binding down the hackle stem and tip should be hidden under the next section , and so on.
DO keep each wrap of chenille firm and close to its neighbour, so that a good tight body that doesn't roll around the hook shank is produced.
DON'T omit to wind thread back over the hackle fibres so they slope back 45° or more to enshroud the body section in a filmy conical veil.
DO remember to leave plenty of room at the end of the shank (B–C) to tie off the head in a neat cone-shape. Too much is better than too little.
DON'T be dismayed if your first few attempts aren't perfect. They will probably be good enough to fool a trout anyway! Practice makes perfect, nothing else, so don't rush, take time with each stage of each fly, and you'll be amazed at the progress you make.

HOW TO USE THE WHIP FINISHER

1. Catch thread between bobbin holder and hook with Part C.
2. Catch thread between C and hook with A.
3. Bring thread between C and bobbin holder behind B. Pull with bobbin holder so unit slides along over thread up to hook. Avoid undue tension on C.
4. Get hook shank behind eye snugly fitted into B,
5. then rotate whip finisher 4 or 5 times until C has stretched forward.
6. Keeping firm pressure on bobbin holder thread, pull whip finisher back from hook far enough to allow A and B to disengage from thread.
7. Pull back with bobbin holder. This will pull C up to hook.
8. Remove C by pulling down and out of thread loop.

You have now made a perfect whip finish. For extra security, repeat sequence once or twice and coat with head cement.

Fig 7
How to use the whip finisher

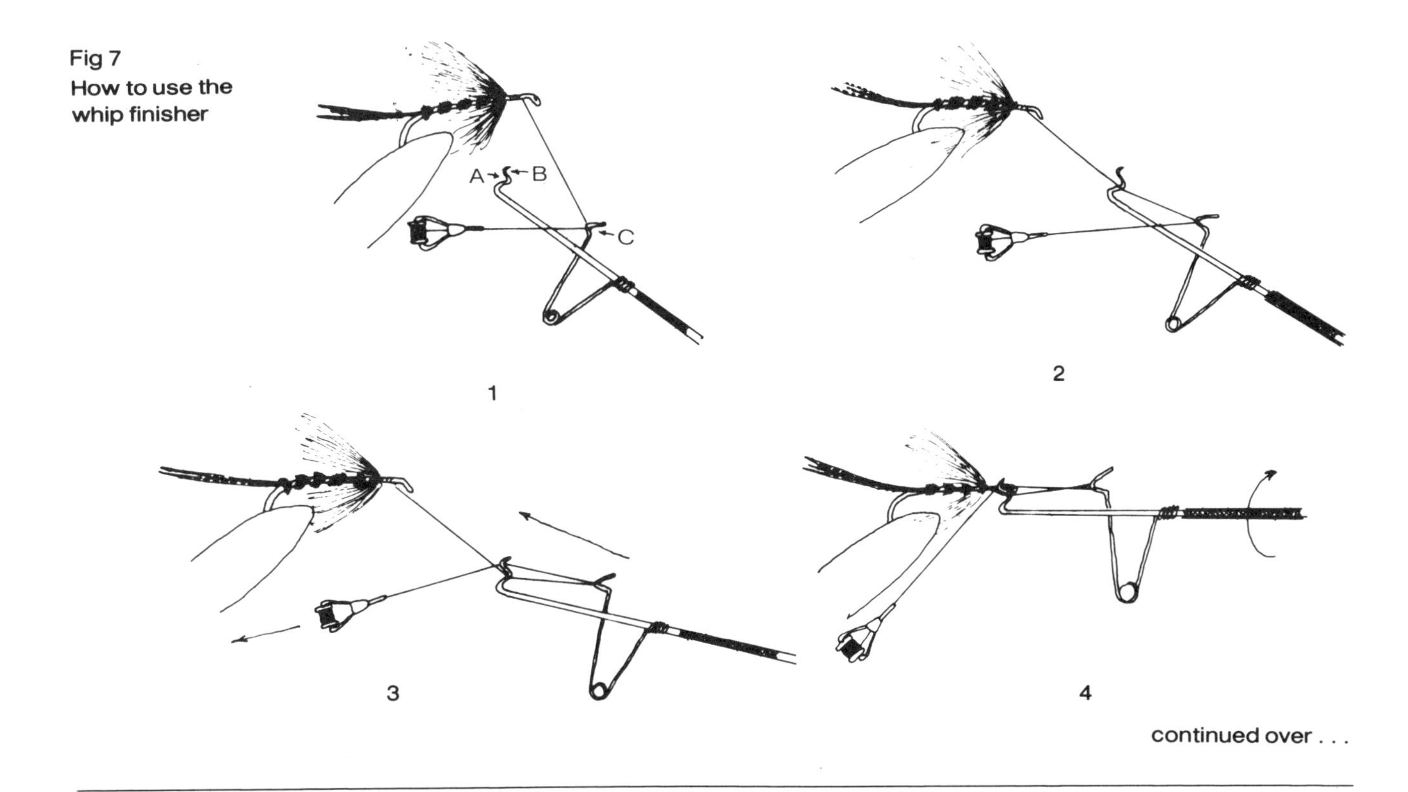

continued over . . .

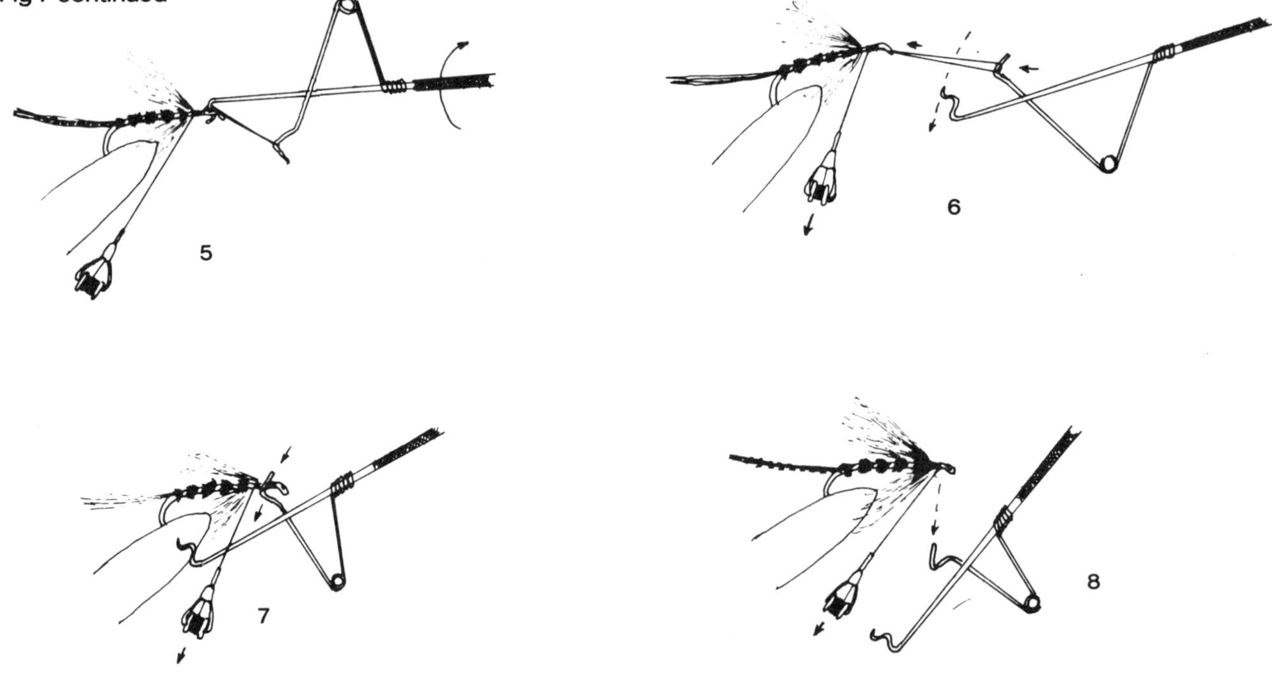
Fig 7 continued
5
6
7
8

HOW TO FINISH OFF WITHOUT A WHIP FINISHER

1. With bobbin holder in left hand, make a loop in thread with fingers of right hand. The length of thread B between hook and forefinger should be *under* the length A from third finger to bobbin holder.
2. Keep A against hook shank and rotate right hand so that B traps A in position.
3. Continue winding B around and over A and shank up to the eye, ensuring wraps are tight.
4. Use a pin or bodkin to keep loop BA tight and to prevent turns from unwinding. Now draw out slack by pulling on A, thus securing B under the wraps. Cinch up tight, trim off surplus and apply head cement.

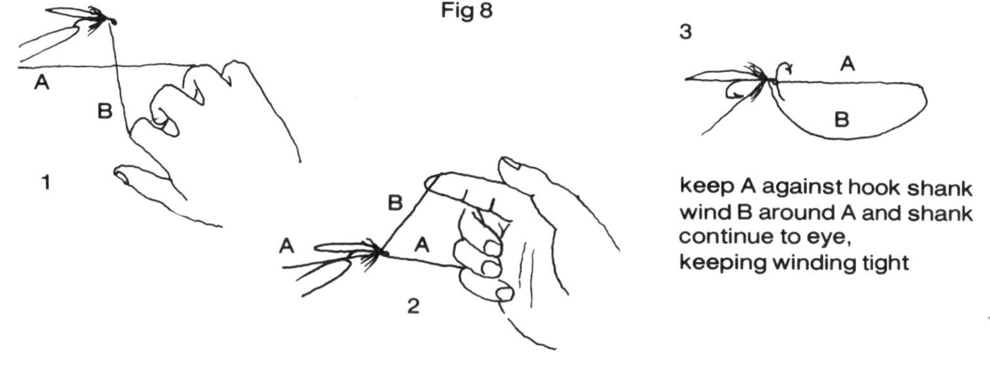

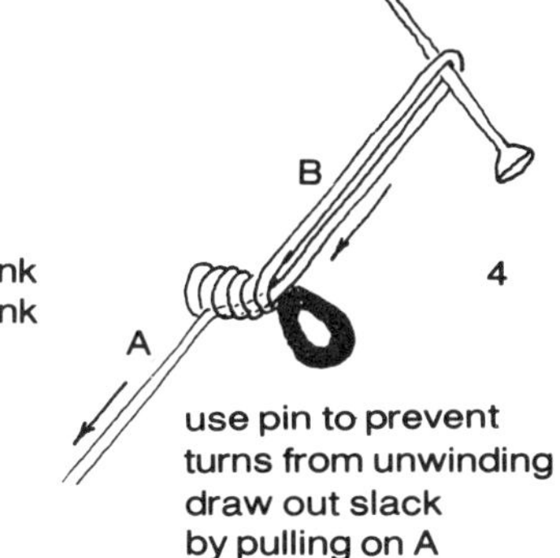

MATUKU-STYLE FLIES

"Matuku" is the Maori word for bittern, and one of the earliest of New Zealand flies was tied using a pair of mottled, soft, long-fibred feathers from this bird, laid back to back and the butts firmly bound in at the head of the fly. A spiral of tinsel running up the body to the head passed at intervals through the hackle fibres and over the central spines, thus securely holding both feathers on edge along the entire length of the top of the fly with the remainder of the feather tips protruding behind.

These "Matukus", as they were called, proved so successful that bitterns were soon being shot by the hundreds to supply the demand for their feathers so, fearing the bird might follow the dodo and the passenger pigeon into extinction, the Government wisely declared it a protected species, along with the kiwi, whose feathers were also being used in a similar fashion. In addition, a complete ban on the use of flies tied with either bird's plumage was imposed, so the pioneers quickly adopted alternative feathers for their Matukus, and the Parson's Glory was certainly one of the earliest of these innovations. Many others followed, including some incorporating totally different wing materials. Partridge tail feathers were split up the centre and sections of both halves used to form a wing in the famous Split Partridge series, while the equally famous Rabbit flies scorned feathers altogether, forming their wings from strips of rabbit skin with fur still attached. But despite the varying ingredients all shared the same unique Matuku method of securing body to wing with spiralling tinsel, and I'd hate to hazard a guess at how many patterns are currently tied in this style.

In the interests of cutting production costs, many of today's commercial tyers leave off the throat hackle and coloured tail fibres that once adorned many of the traditional Matukus. Sometimes I do, too, but for altogether different reasons. Tails on these flies usually consist of bunches of hackle fibres taken from brightly dyed feathers. Sometimes the dyes used aren't colour-fast, and I was dismayed to find many of my flies were developing pink, orange, yellow or green stains where the dye had bled after getting wet, so I tried leaving out the tails on my Matukus altogether. To date it hasn't made any noticeable difference to their effectiveness.

Throat hackle collars I like for purely aesthetic reasons, but I must admit I make these very sparse or omit them completely in some of the very skinny Matuku-style smelt imitations.

One of the most important factors in tying a well-proportioned Matuku is the length of the wing in relation to the body. If it extends too far behind, it will snag round the hook while casting; too short, and the fly won't have the seductive wriggle in the water that it should. In a properly tied Matuku the body should be half the length of the complete fly or, if you prefer, the wing should not extend beyond the end of the body by more than a body-length.

HOW TO TIE A MATUKU-STYLE FLY

1. Bind hook shank with thread from B to A as shown before in step (1) of Hackle fly.
2. If you wish to use a coloured tail, now is the time to tie it in. Take a pinch of red or orange hackle fibres from a dyed feather and secure, using the same technique as (2) in Hackle fly except in this case it should only be about 6–9 mm ($\frac{1}{4}$–$\frac{3}{8}$ in) long when complete.
3. Tie in end of 7.5 cm (3 in) piece of chenille as in (3) for Hackle fly.
4. Tie in end of 7.5 cm (3 in) length of oval tinsel. Trim off surplus.
5. Wind thread back up to B.
6. Wind chenille in close, firm turns up to B, secure with a few turns of thread. Trim off surplus.
7. Take 2 hackles of similar dimensions, pattern and colour. Strip away the fuzz from the bases, plus enough adjacent hackle fibres so as to leave remaining feather approximately twice the length of chenille body.
8. With your left finger and thumb hold both feathers back-to-back, shiny sides out, on edge along top of the chenille-covered hook shank while you bind down the butts securely at B with 5 or 6 turns of thread.
9. Grip protruding feather tips in left finger and thumb and pull lightly back until the stems of both feathers are drawn flat along top of chenille. Using your right hand, gently stroke the hackle fibres along the back forward towards the eye, so they tend to stand up at 90° from the stems, and then wind the tinsel in a tight spiral up the body over the feather stems and between the hackle fibres. Stop at B, secure with a few turns of thread. Trim off surplus tinsel and any feather stems that may be protruding.

Fig 9 How to tie a Matuku-style fly

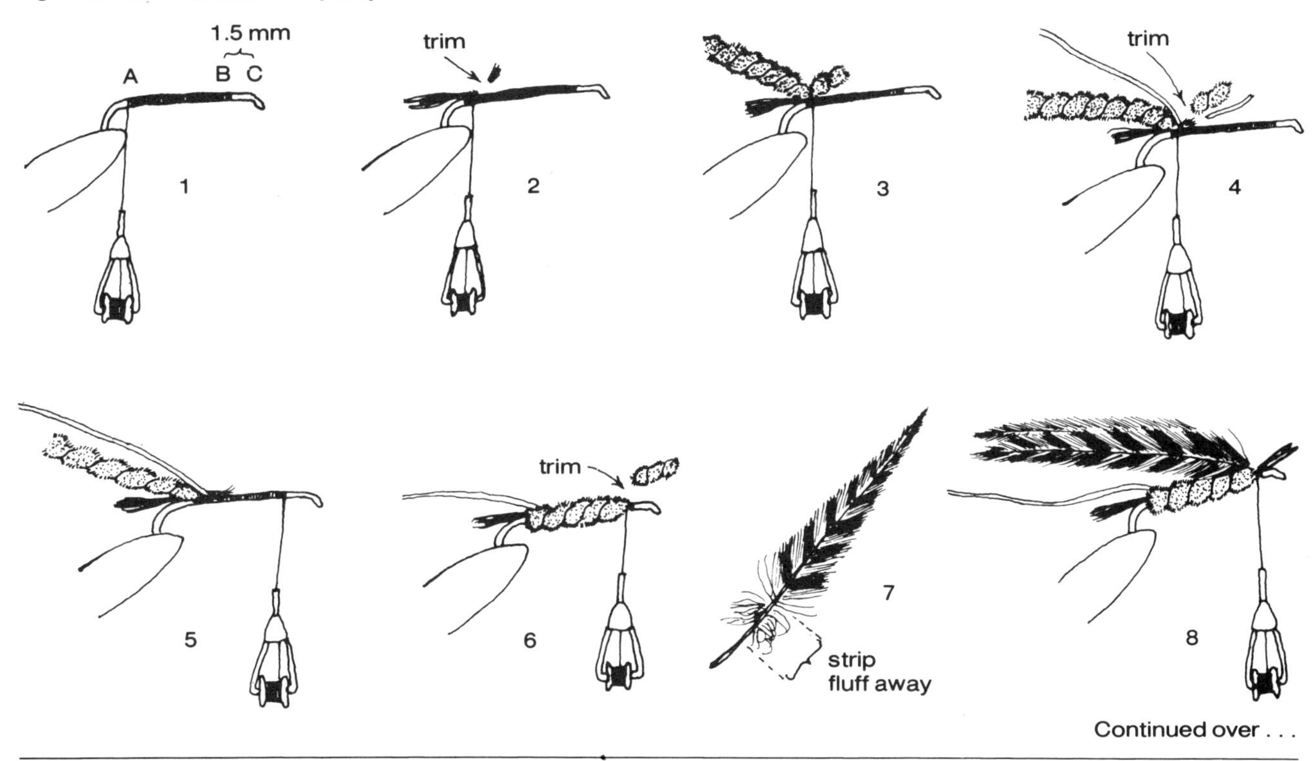

Continued over . . .

Fig 9 continued

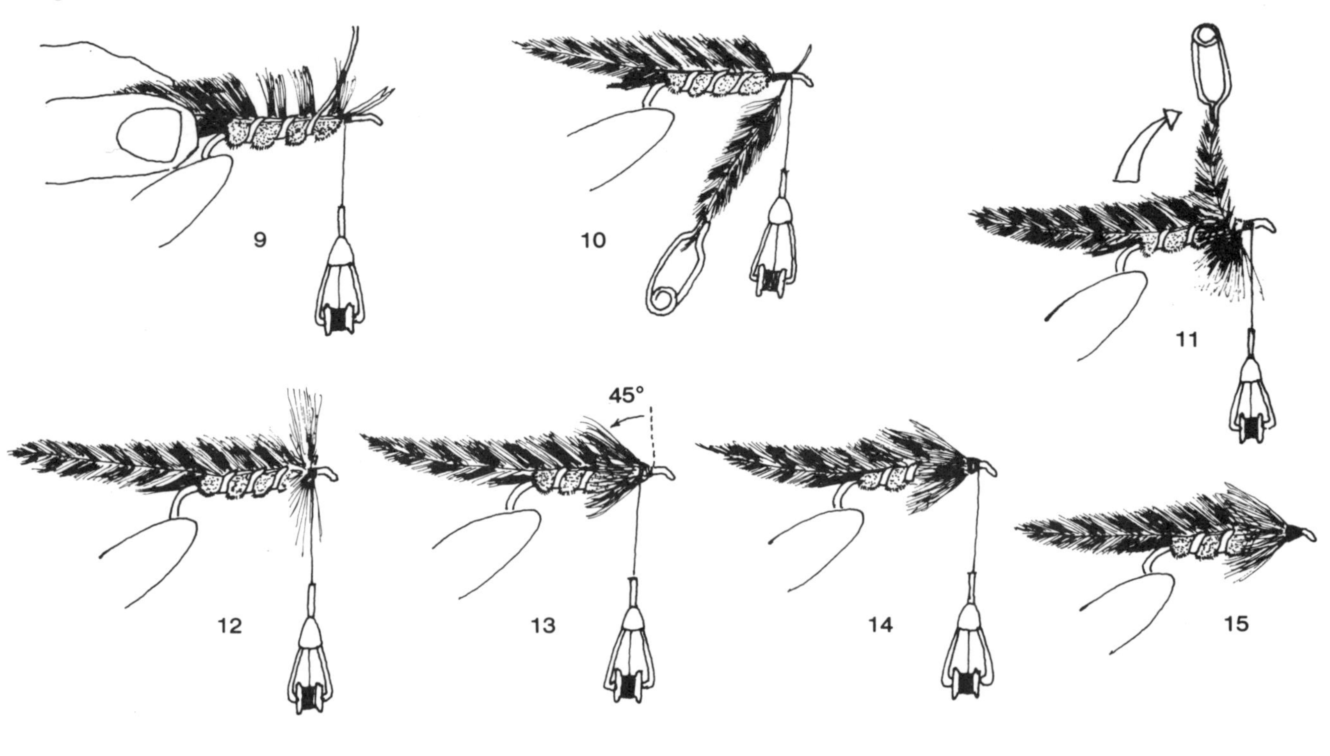

10–14. As mentioned earlier, many tyers prefer to leave out the hackle collar on some Matuku-style flies, particularly small slim smelt patterns like Grey Ghost, for example, so if you like you can jump forward to step (15). However, Parson's Glory and numerous other patterns traditionally call for a hackle collar, so steps (10) to (14) show how to fashion it. You will see it is exactly the same technique as you learned in steps (5) to (9) in the Hackle fly. The feather used is usually the same variety as used for the wings.
15. Whip finish as shown on page 30. Cut the thread, apply head cement to the head and leave to dry for 10 minutes.

If the pattern you are tying calls for a tinsel body (Grey Ghost, Bishop's Blessing, etc.) you may experience some difficulty in securing the ends of the tinsel at steps (3) and (6) in such a way as to avoid ugly bumps or wrinkles. I overcome this problem by cutting the ends at a steep angle, 45° or more. If the tapered cut is facing left when you tie in the tinsel you will find that the winds will automatically want to overlap in a neat spiral all the way up the shank, and since it is tied in at the thinnest part the inevitable bump that occurs is so minuscule as to be invisible. A taper at the other end (facing right), where you secure before trimming off, produces the same neat effect. You'll see exactly what I mean when you try it!

HOW TO TIE A RABBIT FLY

You can see from the illustration that Stages (1) to (5) (the forming of the body) are exactly the same as for the previous Matuku-style pattern. However, instead of a pair of feathers, the wing consists of a strip of rabbit skin with the fur attached. Cut about the width of a matchstick and something similar in length. This is laid along the top of the body, skin-side down of course (with the hair sloping back away from the eye), and secured firmly to the shank with the tying thread at B. The oval tinsel is then spiralled up the body, over the skin and between the hairs, thus holding the strip neatly along the top of the body, tied in at B and surplus trimmed away.

As with other Matuku-style dressings, both tails and hackle collars are optional.

Fig 10

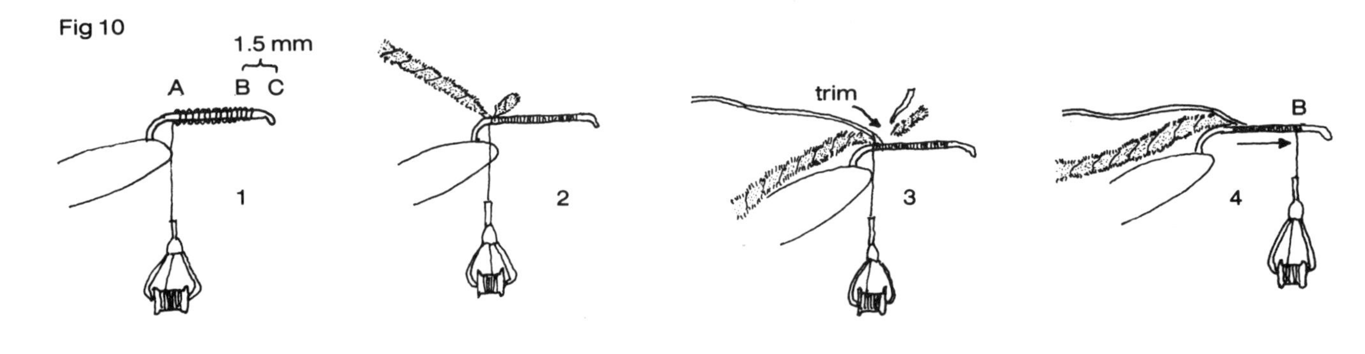

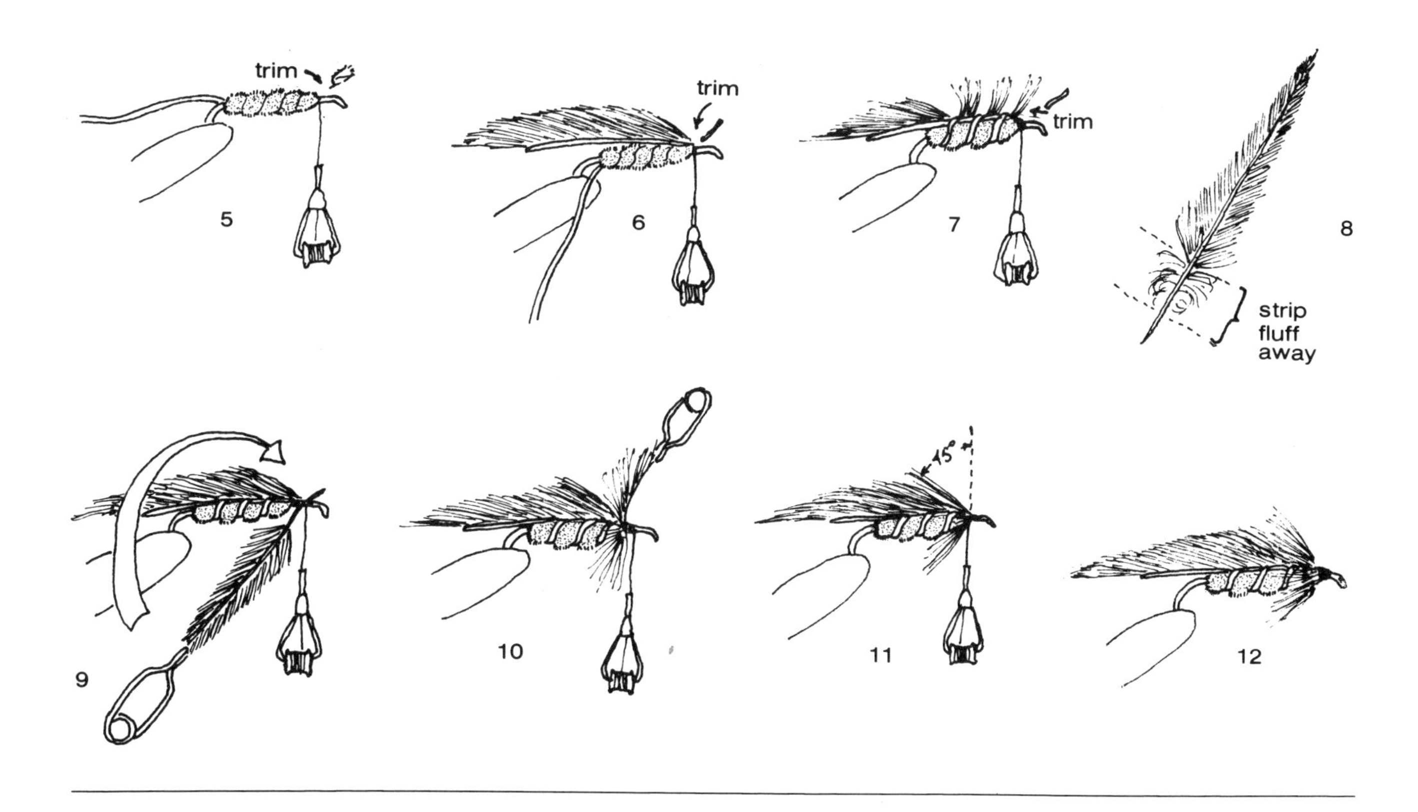
trim
5
trim
6
trim
7
8
strip
fluff
away
9
10
15°
11
12

PUKEKO-STYLE FLIES

Pukekos are New Zealand swamp-dwelling birds whose feathers are usually used in such a way as to form a canopy over the flies that bear their name. I must admit to having a soft spot for these flies, and every time I look at a batch they remind me of so many little portly gentlemen sheltering under their blue or black pukeko umbrellas.

There are five basic popular patterns in the range, Craig's Night-time, Scotch Poacher, Taihape Tickler, Fruit Salad and Black Phantom, and to be honest, I'm not sure exactly what they are supposed to represent, unless maybe it's a great water beetle. But considering that several of them sport red, orange or yellow undersides not found on any great water beetle I've ever come across, I just don't know! Although sometimes effective during daylight, they are really night flies, and I would not have thought the trout would be able to see more than their silhouettes in the dark. Yet the fact remains that sometimes one particular pattern will be chosen more often than any of the others, even on the darkest of nights. I suppose it is one of the many great unsolved mysteries that add to the fascination of fishing.

Of the four basic New Zealand styles of tying, perhaps the Pukeko offers the most unexplored avenues for experiment. A Pukeko fly tied with claret chenille and an orange-red hackle once accounted for a handsome 8-lb (3.6-kg) rainbow hen at Rotorua's Awahou Stream mouth on a still moonlit February night after everyone had gone home because the moon was too bright and I was left with the whole rip to myself. Yet it never ever produced another fish on that or any other night, until eventually I lost it several years later. Maybe when you've mastered all the standard patterns you'd like to try one, if you can ever find claret chenille, that is! Or why not try something in

Red Fuzzy-Wuzzy

Green Fuzzy-Wuzzy

Red Setter

Orange Dappled Dog

Red Taupo Tiger

Parson's Glory

Jack's Sprat

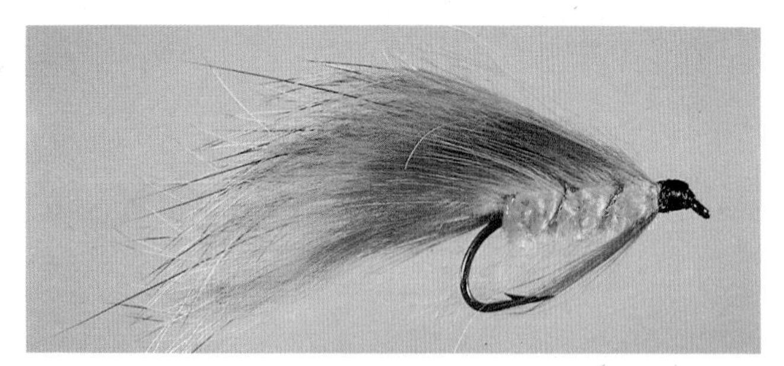

Yellow Rabbit

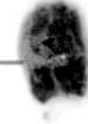

MATUKU-STYLE LURES

perhaps a green body and black hackles with Hamill's plumage on top? Mallard, pheasant and paradise duck feathers, too, all have their possibilities if used in lieu of pukeko but tied in the Pukeko style. Who knows, you may even come up with a new and deadly pattern all your own!

HOW TO TIE A PUKEKO-STYLE FLY

1. Bind the shank with thread.
2. Tie in tail exactly as for a Hackle-style fly. If the pattern calls for a short wool tag tail instead, leave approximately 6 mm ($\frac{1}{4}$ in) of the wool protruding, and when this has been secured, tease it out into a fluffy tag with your bodkin.
3. Tie in chenille and oval tinsel as you did for the Matuku-style fly.
4. Wind chenille up the shank to form a body. Secure at B and trim surplus.
5. Wind the tinsel in a spiral over the body, secure at B and trim surplus.
6. There are actually three courses you can take at this stage. In the method illustrated, having removed the fuzz and fibres from the two similar pukeko feathers, you bind each of them by the butt at B, one on top of the other so they form a canopy over the body, then tie in a hackle feather as in step (7). Wind it round the shank to form a hackle collar, secure the top and trim away the surplus before winding the thread back so the fibres are swept back to 45°.
   The alternative method is to go on to step (7), i.e., tie in the hackle collar first and *then* secure the pukeko feathers over the top.
   The third choice is to finish off at (6) and so leave the hackle off altogether, a technique favoured by many successful veteran anglers in the Rotorua district. I suggest you try all three, and stick to the one you find most successful!
8. Whip finish, cut thread, apply head cement and hang up to dry.

Incidentally, the number of pukeko feathers used for the wing in my illustration is two, but I have seen as many as six used, depending on the whim of the individual tyer. Try and keep the feathers aligned with the body, not bulging out too far at the sides and not protruding more than 6 mm ($\frac{1}{4}$ in) beyond the bend of the hook.

Fig 11 How to tie a Pukeko-style fly

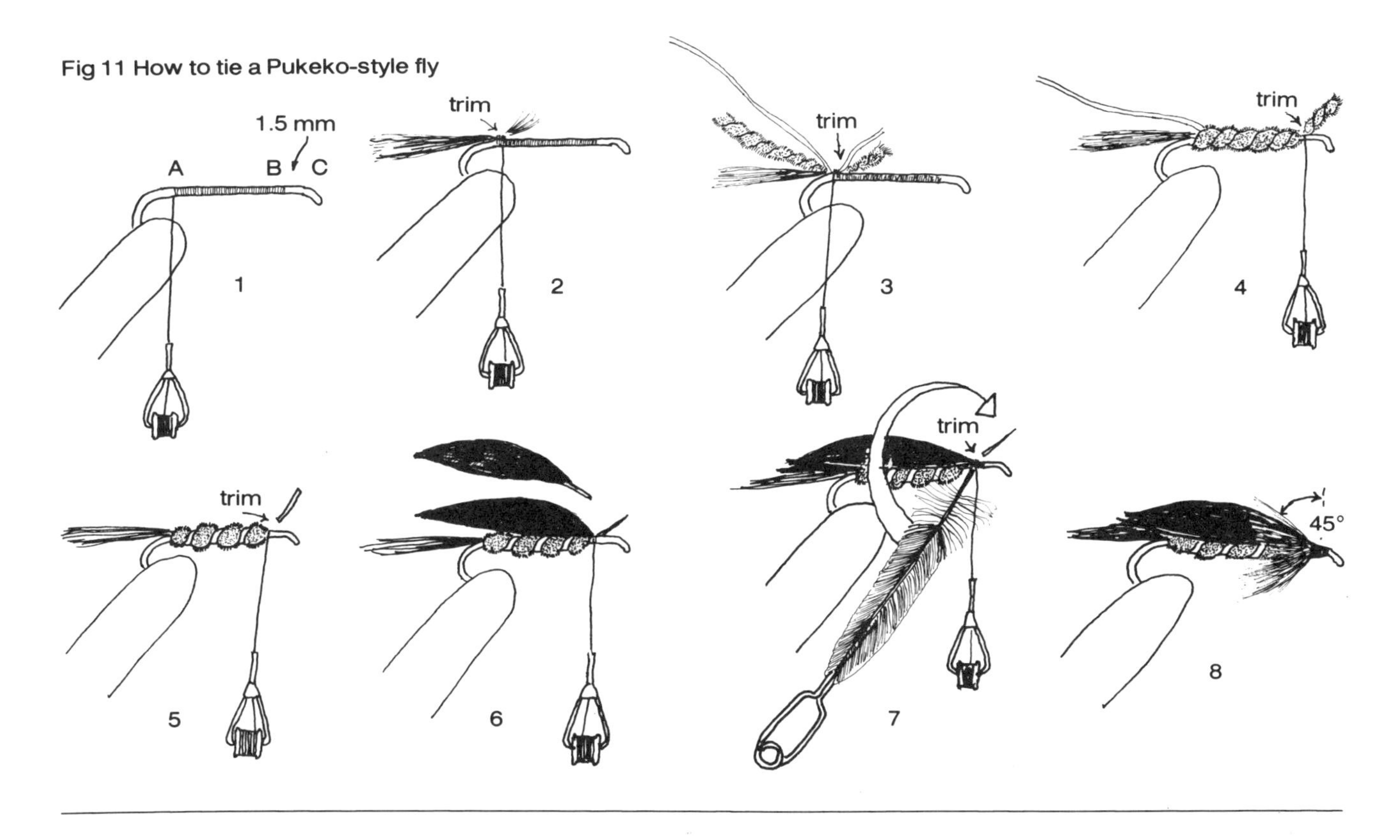

KILLER-STYLE FLIES

While the Killer style may not be the easiest method to master, it certainly isn't impossible, and there is no doubt that killer flies can be extremely effective when it comes to the capture of big trout.

There are about ten members of the family currently in vogue; Mrs Simpson, Mallard, Hamill's Killer, Kilwell No. 1 and Kilwell No. 2, each tied with a red or yellow body. Since the body is completely hidden inside the completed fly, I have never been able to fathom how the colour could possibly have any bearing on its success, but old traditions die hard, and you'll find Killers almost inevitably have either red or yellow bodies.

The construction of a Killer differs from other flies in that the feathers are tied in on the *sides* of the body. When properly tied, the shape is basically oval with a little tail protruding at the end. The feathers should overlap smoothly to produce slightly swelling sides, and the edges of the opposing feathers should meet all the way along, leaving no gap at the top or bottom of the fly. If you visualise a small almond with a tail, you'll get the idea of what I mean.

Many of the old patterns like Spa Special, Leslie's Lure and Lord's Killer have all but disappeared for one reason or another but, despite the difficulties of construction, people still experiment. George Gatchell of Waitahanui once gave me some beautifully tied Killers made from paradise duck feathers, and I recently saw a striking specimen utilising the yellow and black barred feathers from a deceased pet budgie's neck! Some interesting results can also be obtained with California quail plumage, which produces a pleasing marbled effect in tones of grey, cream and black, but alas the feathers are delicate and the flies tend to come apart after very little use.

To be completely honest, I don't particularly like tying Killers. They are awkward, fiddly, exasperating, time-consuming things to construct, and if I were tying commercially I should charge triple the going rate for them. However don't let this put you off. Persevere and eventually you'll get one to come out just right, and believe me the satisfaction in this achievement will make it all seem worthwhile. If you should ever by any chance hit upon an easy method of tying them, please let me know, but in the interim, any time I come across a particularly neatly tied, beautifully proportioned, well-balanced specimen, I will buy it, for a good Killer is "a thing of beauty and a joy for ever", and every fly-box should have some.

HOW TO TIE A KILLER-STYLE FLY

The first four steps are exactly the same as those used in (1) to (4) for a Hackle fly except that I prefer to use wool rather than the more bulky chenille.

5. Remove fluff and fibres from the bottom ends of the two matching feathers.
6. Bind one by the stem (concave in) to the side of the shank so the spine of the feather is in line with the body and the feather hides most of the hook bend and part of the tail. Repeat on the opposite side so both feathers are exactly the same length, cupping the body between them like a sandwich.

7–9. Repeat steps (3) to (6).

10. Whip finish, cut thread, apply cement and hang to dry.

Killers are dreadful things to tie, so don't be dismayed if you don't master the art right away. One of the secrets is to make sure each feather is secured *exactly* the way you want it before going on to the next one, even if it means winding and unwinding a dozen times to get it right. When I get one to lie correctly I sometimes put a drop of clear head cement round the base and wait for it to set hard before proceeding, lest the subsequent activity disturbs it. Ideally the top and bottom edges of the opposing feathers should meet, but so long as the tops do I don't think the bottom matters that much. In fact, some of the more knowledgeable Rotorua pundits prefer a little of the body to show on the underside. The general shape, too, is a matter of opinion. Some like a fat head and a tapering body, necessitating the use of different sizes of feathers, while others prefer an oval shape or a long slender profile. Whatever your choice this is one pattern you will really have to work at before you perfect it. Just be glad the pattern has simplified over the years; some of the old dressings I've seen called for three sets of feathers, three deep on each side – 18 in all. The mind boggles!

Fig 12 How to tie a Killer-style fly

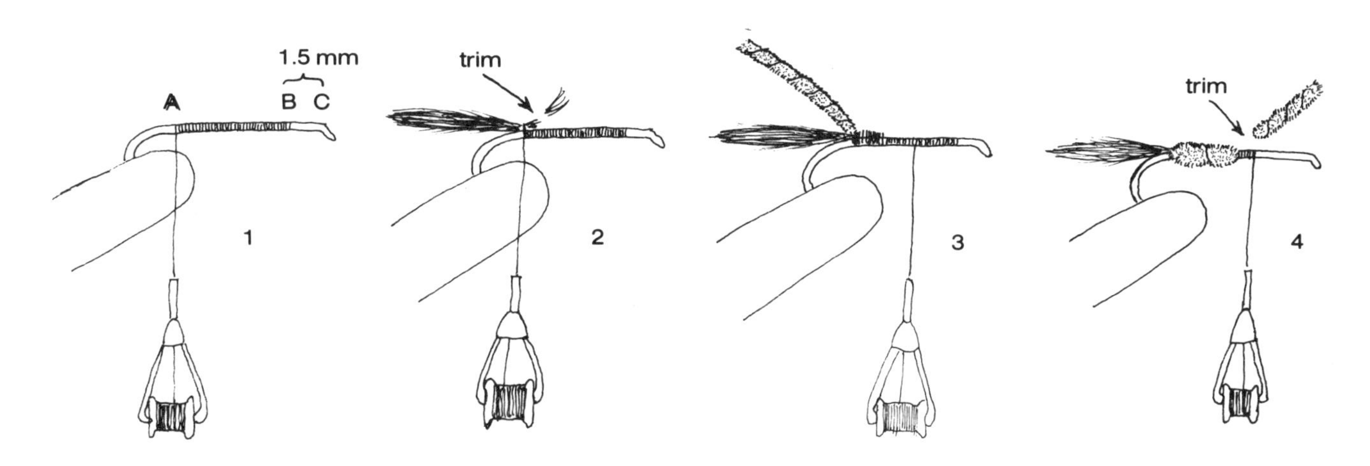

Continued over . . .

Fig 12 continued

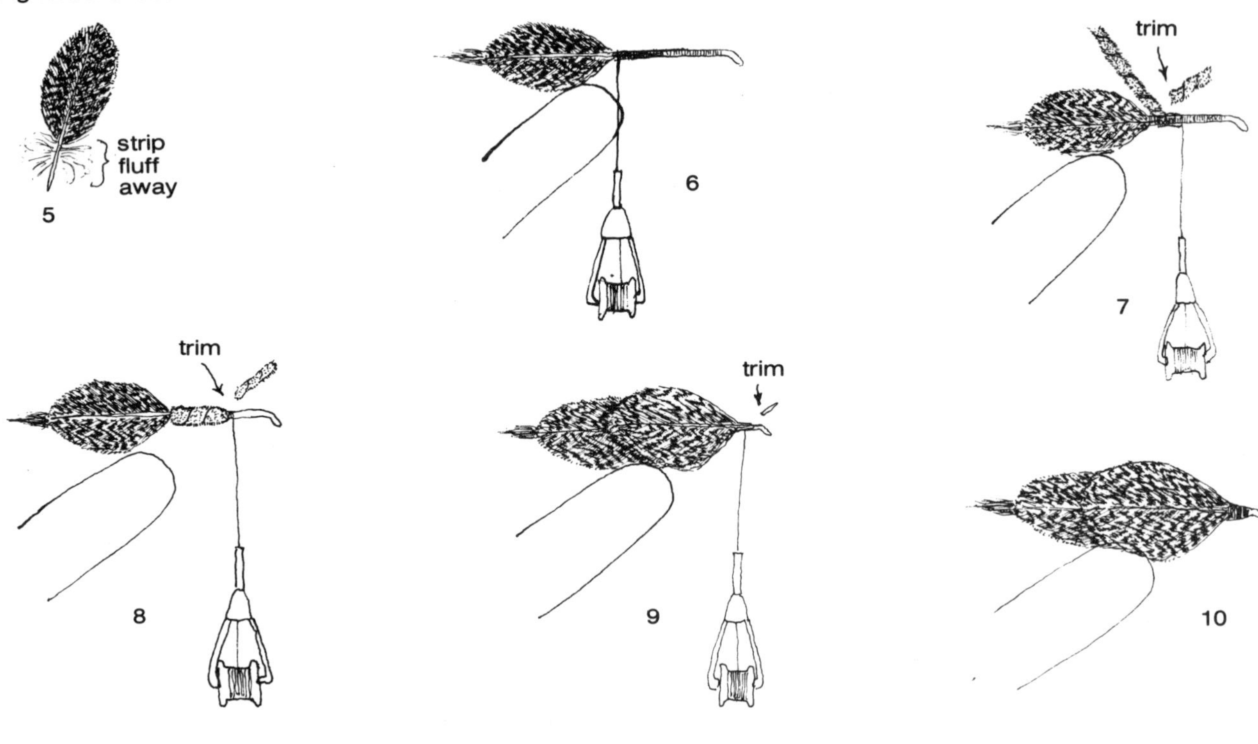

GUIDE TO N.Z. LURE PATTERNS

The initial of the tying style is shown in brackets after the name of the pattern thus:

HACKLE = (H)
MATUKU = (M)
PUKEKO = (P)
KILLER = (K)

BISHOP'S BLESSING (M)

Body: flat silver Mylar
Tail: (optional) bunch of yellow hackle fibres
Tinsel: oval silver
Wings: honey grizzle cock hackles
Hackle collar: (optional) honey grizzle cock hackle

This is really little other than a silver-bodied Parson's Glory and in fact is sometimes referred to as a Silver Parson's. It is a good summer harling fly for Lake Rotorua and, as my wife will attest, also works well when tied with a gold body.

BLACK MATUKA (M)

(See BLACK PRINCE)

BLACK PHANTOM (K)

Body: black or red chenille
Tail: black squirrel tail
Tinsel: oval silver
Wings: black pukeko feathers

This is a relatively new fly whose only claim to the name Black Phantom is that it uses the same materials as the much older original, which was tied not as a Killer, but in the Pukeko style (see below).

BLACK PHANTOM (P)

Body: black or red chenille
Tail: black squirrel tail fibres (sometimes tied on top of a red wool tag)
Tinsel: silver oval
Wings: black pukeko feathers
Hackle collar: none

BLACK PRINCE (M)

Body: black or red chenille
Tail: (optional) bunch of dyed red hackle fibres
Tinsel: oval silver
Wings: dyed black cock hackles
Hackle collar: dyed black cock hackles

If there were a prize for the fly with the most names, the Black Prince would have to be a leading contender. The black-bodied version of this New Zealand night fly is also known as an All Black and in the South Island the red-bodied one is sometimes called Hart's Creek. In Australia, America and Great Britain there is the Black Matuka and the Red Matuka which, despite too-short wings, are tied in the Matuku style and are unquestionably Black Princes. Curiously, our overseas friends regard them highly as flies for daytime use; are we perhaps missing out by regarding them only as night flies?

CRAIG'S NIGHT-TIME (P)

Body: black chenille
Tail: small tag of red wool
Tinsel: oval silver
Wings: black or blue pukeko feathers
Hackle collar: black

This is one pattern which has really evolved radically since its creation in the thirties. The original featured a dark blue body with pale blue hackle as far as I can determine and had two golden pheasant crests, one upturned above the red tail, the other sweeping back down over the wing from the head, while a pair of jungle cock "eyes" completed the fly. Over the years the body and hackle changed to black and the golden crests disappeared along with the jungle cock eyes. For a time some tyers used a single jungle cock eye laid on top of the wing. Eventually that was replaced with a small bunch of yellow hackle fibres, but nowadays even that seems to be vanishing and you will often find Craigs tied today without hackle either. Strangely enough, despite all the alterations and omissions, it continues to be a rattling good night fly and is exceedingly popular throughout the country.

DAPPLED DOG (H)

Body: fluorescent orange or lime chenille
Tail: grey squirrel tail fibres
Hackle: grizzle cock hackles

Designed by Geoff Sanderson of Turangi, these flies can be singularly effective on fresh-run rainbows, often when all other patterns fail. Their secret *appears* to be in the fluorescent material used in their bodies glowing through the thin grey veils of the hackle, but who knows for certain?

DISCO DOLL (H)

Body: a violent shocking pink chenille marketed as "fluorescent red"
Tail: grey squirrel tail or white hackle fibres
Hackles: white cock hackles

This is one Hackle fly you're *not* likely to come across in the average tackle shop but, since it is simple to tie and once or twice has been known to work wonders, I have included it in this list. I don't know who the inventor was; for a while I once thought *I* was, until I later saw someone else using "my" invention.

One bleak drizzly June afternoon, after a fruitless morning on the Tongariro, I came across an American fisherman struggling along with a string of hefty trout. He told me that he too had been drawing a blank until, in despair, he'd tied on a "good ole Yankee shad fly", and this had accounted for seven fish before the hook broke. Since he didn't have another one like it, and nothing else seemed to be working, he was heading back to his motel, having had enough action for one day anyway, he said. He showed me the bedraggled remains of his successful fly. The body was the most lurid shade of fluorescent, shocking pink, with a few straggly wisps of white hackle tied in at the throat, and a couple of bead-chain segments secured above provided a pair of "bug-eyes".

Back at camp that night, I tied up some Hackle-style lures along the lines of a Dappled Dog, but using white cock hackles and a shocking pink chenille (which for some reason is marketed as "fluorescent red"). I left the eyes off, partly because I didn't have any bead-chain and partly because I feared their addition might be classed as "artificial weighting" and therefore illegal!

Next day I tried them out and took a limit of good fish which was particularly rewarding since nobody else I met that day was having any luck at all. That evening, flushed with the success of my invention, I was dismantling my tackle at the car in the dusk, when a small Maori boy appeared through the lupin dragging an enormous brownie. When I went over to congratulate him, he opened the boot of his father's car and shyly showed me five other trout he'd caught earlier, including two mind-blowing browns which must have been in the double figures. And his fly? Yes, you've guessed it, the same one I'd "invented" the previous night! Got it from his dad, he said . . . .

On my next visit to the Tongariro I found that everyone seemed to be using the Disco Doll as I learned it was now called, and everyone was catching fish, but as the months passed its fish-catching ability seemed to fade and by the end of the season it was just another fly.

I've never had any dramatic repeats of the early success I enjoyed with the Disco Doll, but I still carry a couple in my fly box, just in case I might ever find myself fishless on the Tongariro again on a drizzly June afternoon.

Incidentally, Barry Grieg of Turangi showed me a variation of this pattern which has recently made a big impact on the local fishing scene, differing from the Disco Doll only in that the second segment of chenille used is hot orange instead of shocking pink and the white hackles are extremely sparse. It's called Louie's Lure, and for a while I thought that perhaps there had been some mix-up between the names "Louie" and "Hughie" but, alas, no. It seems the creator is in fact an American who comes here each winter just to fish the Tongariro, and sometimes I wonder if by any chance he's the same American who first showed me his "good ole Yankee shad fly" all those years ago!

DOROTHY (M)

Body: red, yellow or green chenille or flat silver Mylar
Tail: (on silver one only) bunch red dyed hackle fibres
Tinsel: oval silver

Wings: grizzle cock hackles
Hackle collar: (optional) grizzle cock hackle

Although all the Dorothys are popular, my favourite is undoubtedly the silver-bodied one. In the larger sizes it is an excellent choice for harling, while tied without a hackle collar on a small No. 8 or even No. 10 hook, it can be very effective when cast to smelting fish.

FRUIT SALAD (P)

Body: equal portions red, black and yellow chenille
Tail: bunch dyed yellow cock hackle fibres
Tinsel: (optional) oval silver
Wings: blue or black pukeko feathers
Hackle collar: dyed orange or black

This is a night fly which, as you can see, has a lot of alternative dressings, all of which seem to be currently in use, and I have not been able to determine what constitutes the original combination. This includes the order in which the tri-coloured body should be arranged. I can only suggest you try them all and stick to the one that works best for you.

FUZZY-WUZZY (H)

Body: hot orange, red, yellow, green or black chenille
Tail: black squirrel tail fibres
Hackle: dyed black cock hackles

Although mainly used after dark, the Fuzzy-Wuzzy often works well during the day, too. I imagine the general shape, silhouette and movement of the hackles combine to create the illusion of a freshwater koura (crayfish).

Everyone has his own favourite body colour (mine being orange), but since the trout sometimes have their own ideas, and since it's such an easy fly to tie, perhaps it's best to carry some of each, just in case.

GINGER MICK (M)

Body: red chenille
Tail: (optional) bunch dyed yellow hackle fibres
Tinsel: oval silver
Wings: ginger cock hackle
Hackle collar: (optional) ginger cock hackle

The Ginger Mick is a reasonably good general all-purpose lure, and I never thought of it as anything other than "just another fly" until I met Dave McLellan of Tisdalls in Auckland. Dave ties his Ginger Micks with the long slender hackles you get in really top-quality capes sold for tying dry flies (both in ginger and furnace), over a red wool, not chenille, body on a No.8 hook. There is no hackle collar, and the wings extend twice as far as normal in a Matuku-style dressing, but they don't foul the hook when casting as frequently as you would imagine, due to the stiff characteristics of this type of feather.

The resultant skinny, wriggly fly can be absolutely deadly on trout packed up at the cold stream mouths of Lake Rotorua in warm weather. Try it and see for yourself.

GREEN ORBIT (M)

Body: green chenille
Tail: bunch of dyed orange or yellow hackle fibres
Tinsel: oval silver
Wings: dyed green grizzle cock hackle
Hackle collar: (optional) dyed green grizzle cock hackle

This is particularly popular as a harling fly and in smaller sizes it is a fair imitation of the greenish fast-swimming damsel fly nymphs, so it's a good choice for weedy lakes where these trout food items abound in the summer months.

GREY GHOST (M)

Body: flat silver Mylar
Tail: (optional) bunch dyed red or grey hackle fibres
Tinsel: oval silver
Wings: dyed grey cock hackle
Hackle collar: (optional) dyed grey cock hackle

A silver-bodied Grey Ghost is certainly one of the finest smelt imitations there is. Large ones for harling can have a lightly dressed "one-wind" collar hackle, but I leave the hackle off completely when I tie the smaller numbers designed to be cast at smelting trout.

An alternative version, tied with a fluorescent lime chenille or wool body, has quite a large following in the Taupo area, but personally I have not had any dramatic results with it. However, I *have* found that the shade of feather used for the wing is important and can make quite a difference, so I usually carry a few variations ranging from almost sooty grey to nearly white among my regular Grey Ghosts.

HAMILL'S KILLER (K)

Body: black squirrel tail fibres
Tail: red or yellow chenille or wool
Sides: grey partridge feathers dyed a pea-green shade

For some reason this pattern originally had a small bunch of golden pheasant tippet fibres tied in on top of the squirrel tail, but this adornment has virtually disappeared today. Another change that has occurred in recent years has been brought about by the shortage and high cost of grey partridge feathers, and many Hamill's Killers are now tied with suitably dyed grey mallard flank feathers instead.

In larger sizes Hamill's Killers probably represent a big greenish bully, while smaller sizes may be taken for dragonfly nymphs, but whatever they represent they are extremely effective lures and form a very useful addition to any fly box.

HART'S CREEK (M)

(see BLACK PRINCE)

Craig's Night-time

Scotch Poacher

Taihape Tickler

Black Phantom

Hybrid Mrs Simpson (Church Window Feathers)

Hamill's Killer

Kilwell No. 1

Mrs Simpson

KILLER-STYLE LURES

JACK'S SPRAT (M)

Body: flat silver Mylar
Tail: none
Tinsel: oval silver
Wings: badger cock hackles
Hackle collar: (optional) badger cock hackle

> A man called Spratt and his good wife
> Both had opposing taste.
> When they got stuck into a feed
> Nothing went to waste.
> They had a fly named after them,
> The best I've ever seen,
> With badger wing white-striped with fat
> O'er silver body lean.

Or so goes the old jingle anyway. Being little more than a Grey Ghost tied with badger feathers, the same suggestions on hackle collars apply, i.e., tie sparsely for large sizes and leave off altogether on the small ones.

A rattling good smelt fly, the Jack's Sprat, though I'm surprised that by now some enterprising Taupo fly-dresser hasn't come up with a lime-bodied version!

KILWELL No. 1 (K)

Body: red or yellow chenille or wool
Tail: black squirrel tail fibres
Sides: brown partridge feathers with white stripe

For my money this is one of the very best of the Killer patterns and is certainly one that no fisherman should be without.

I was first introduced to the fly by Geoff Thomas, the leading Rotorua guide, many years ago at Lake Tarawera, and since then it would have accounted for more of the trout I've caught there than all others put together.

Like all Killers, it is not simple to tie, but this one is doubly difficult since ideally the side feathers have to all be arranged so that the white stripes form a continuous line down the entire length of the fly.

Developed by Frank Lord of Rotorua, it was originally called the Tarawera Killer.

KILWELL No. 2 (K)

Body: red or yellow chenille or wool
Tail: black squirrel tail fibres
Sides: speckled sepia and black feathers from European grouse

Although grouse feathers were not always in as short supply as they appear to be today, the Kilwell No. 2 has never enjoyed the popularity it should have despite the fact that it is an excellent lure for both night and day use, being especially good at the change of light.

This fly seems to be *particularly* effective at Lake Rerewhakaaitu (between Rotorua and Murupara), for reasons best known to the rainbows that reside there!

Another of Frank Lord's creations, this was originally named Rotoiti Killer.

LIME PARSON'S (M)

(See PARSON'S GLORY)

LORD'S KILLER (K)

Body: yellow or red chenille or wool
Tail: black squirrel tail fibres
Sides: mottled woodcock plumage

The woodcock's delicate mottled plumage contains every shade of brown from darkest sepia to palest fawn, and a Lord's Killer therefore looks singularly like a bully, one of the lake-dwelling trout's favourite foods. Unfortunately, woodcock feathers have become nearly impossible to find over the last few years, so alas Lord's Killers have all but vanished from the angling scene nowadays.

Although I've shown wool or chenille as the proper body material, I have in my possession some specimens tied by the originator, Mr Frank Lord of Rotorua, who incidentally also developed the Taihape Tickler mentioned on p.68. The bodies of these originals are of a coarse hairy yellowish material which I couldn't for the life of me identify, so I asked Frank what it was. He laughed and said it was either from the stuffing of an old saddle or the felt pad that lies under it, and he'd chosen that because he liked the colour and the texture of it and he had a plentiful supply available at the time.

Since neither of these materials is easy to get hold of, I've used rough yellowish dubbed fur for bodies of the few Lord's Killers I've tied. I don't know whether it makes any difference to the completed fly or not, but when someone speaks who's caught as many big trout as Frank Lord has, I listen!

LOUIE'S LURE (H)

(See DISCO DOLL)

MALLARD (K)

Body: red or yellow chenille or wool
Tail: black or grey squirrel tail fibres
Sides: the finely barred black and white feather known as "grey mallard flank"

Despite its bulky profile, this fly makes a good smelt imitation because when wet, the fibres of the mallard feathers tend to collapse and, sweeping back, give the fly a much more streamlined, fish-like appearance.

For this reason I have often thought it might be a good idea to tie some Mallards with silver Mylar bodies which would glint and flash through the undulating feather fibres, but somehow I've never got around to it yet!

Yet another of Geoff Sanderson's creations.

MATUKU (M)

Body: red, yellow, orange or green chenille
Tail: none
Tinsel: oval silver
Wings: soft feathers from hen pheasant flank or body

When many years ago a ban was placed on the use of flies made from bittern feathers, sportsmen eagerly sought alternative materials for their Matukus. The dressing shown here was among the first attempts, although mohair or seal's fur was commonly used for the bodies in those early dressings.

Not a very popular fly nowadays, but you still come across one now and again, so I have included it in the list. Do not confuse with the patterns tied overseas bearing the name Matuka (see Black Prince).

MRS SIMPSON (K)

Body: red or yellow chenille or wool
Tail: black squirrel tail fibres
Sides: cock pheasant rump feathers

This fly got its name from the lady for whom Edward VIII gave up the English throne, the suggestion probably being that if one Mrs Simpson could catch the King of England, another could be expected to hook the King of the Lake!

Originally tied with the greenish-fringed rump feathers from a cock pheasant, today Mrs Simpson is frequently dressed with the chocolate and cream "church-window" feather found further up the back of the bird.

Dressed either way, it is a good choice of pattern for both day and night fishing.

PARSON'S GLORY (M)

Body: yellow chenille
Tail: (optional) bunch of red or orange fibres from dyed cock hackle
Tinsel: gold or silver oval tinsel
Wings: honey grizzle cock hackle
Hackle collar: honey grizzle cock hackle

According to Kelly's of Rotorua Parson's Glory is the second most popular fly in the country, being fractionally behind Red Setter and just ahead of Hamill's Killer.

It is a beautiful fly to look at, and although the traditional dressings of golden pheasant crest and jungle cock eyes have long since been dropped and the mohair body replaced with chenille, it is still a masterpiece in skilfully blended shades of buff, ginger, yellow and gold.

I must have caught hundreds of trout on the Parson's Glory, but one in particular will always stand out in my memory. My wife and I were casting from an anchored dinghy on Lake Okataina when I hooked a powerful fish which took off in a wild uncontrollable fashion, ripping line from my madly protesting reel at a frightening rate. I was using an old floppy Hardy split-cane rod which bent at an alarming angle as I exerted all the pressure I dared, but to no avail; in no time at all the backing line had gone, and if we hadn't been able to follow the fish in the dinghy, that, as they say, would have been that.

However, Dame Fortune smiled on me and after a long tussle I eventually netted a superb rainbow hen of 5½ lb (2.5 kg) which, being only 19½ in (44.5 cm) long, had a condition factor of 74. Being one of the best-conditioned fish I'd ever taken up to then, I quickly administered the last rites, removed the fly and held the trout up for a photograph when I noticed the fly was still attached to its jaw. Closer examination showed that the first Parson's Glory I'd extracted wasn't the one I'd caught it on at all, but one that had already been left there following a previous encounter we'd had some weeks earlier. I was able to identify the fly as being one of my own creations by the unusually marked variant feathers I'd used for the wings and a unique stain at the end of the body where dye from the orange tail had run. What the odds are against hooking the same fish twice in a body of water the size of Lake Okataina I don't know, but they must be astronomical.

RABBIT (M)

Wing:	strip of natural rabbit	black rabbit
Tinsel:	oval silver	oval gold
Body:	red, green, yellow or orange chenille; or flat silver Mylar	black chenille
Tail:	yellow, orange or red	red or orange
Hackle collar:	ginger or grizzle	black

The Rabbit is unquestionably one of my favourite lures, but because the pattern calls for a strip of rabbit (or feral cat!) pelt in lieu of feathers, some people may question its inclusion as a Matuku-style fly. However, I have done so because, regardless of the material used, the *method* of attaching the wing to the body with a spiral of tinsel remains the same. Rabbits are among the most versatile of flies. By using different hook sizes, varying the body colours and experimenting with assorted lengths, widths and shades of pelt, you can produce anything from a big koura or leech imitation to tiny suggestions of damsel fly nymphs or smelt.

Rabbit flies are great fish catchers, and you have only to watch the action of one in the water to see why. The wing wriggles, writhes and flutters in a most lifelike manner as the fly darts about in the current, but it won't do this until the stiff dry skin has soaked up enough water to become limp and flexible. This is the reason you rarely get a strike first cast after tying on a rabbit. I say "rarely" because, paradoxically, I'm reminded of a curious thing that once happened to me.

I arrived at the Lonely Pool on the Tongariro one morning only to find another angler already fishing it, so sitting down on the stones at the head of the pool to await my turn, I selected a Rabbit from my box, knotted it on the leader and dropped it in the water at my feet to soak. As I hunched over to light a cigarette, my rod was jerked violently from my lap and a beautiful fat rainbow hen sprang into the air in front of me amid a welter of spray. I seized the rod and leapt to my feet, there was a savage tug that dragged the tip underwater, then she was gone taking my fly with her. On examining the leader I found it was neatly secured to the rod tip by no less than two half hitches, so either she was an instructor in some piscine guide troop or she came from a particularly nautical strain of trout! However, I suppose the lesson to be learned from all this is not so much the efficiency of the Rabbit, wet or otherwise, as the importance of fishing the water close to you before you go wading into the deeps.

RED MATUKA (M) (See BLACK PRINCE)

RED SETTER (H)

Body: hot orange chenille
Tail: black or red squirrel tail fibres
Hackle: ginger cock hackles

This fly was originally developed by Geoff Sanderson of Turangi and is probably the best-known and most popular pattern in New Zealand today.

It's a great all-round fly, for while it is particularly effective on migrating pre-spawning rainbows, it can also be successfully used for both harling and curiously, night fishing.

As well as being a grand fish-producer, it is a very photogenic pattern, and a single specimen glowing in the jaw of a freshly-landed trout, or a whole radiant boxful included in a still-life study, has made many a colour slide come alive.

Should squirrel tail be in short supply, the new synthetic FisHair in either brown or black makes an acceptable substitute.

ROTODYERAN SPECIAL (H)

Body: fluorescent lime chenille
Tail: black squirrel tail
Hackles: dyed yellow and grizzle cock hackles

This pattern is one you are probably unfamiliar with, and it's highly unlikely you'll ever find it listed among New Zealand's top ten most popular flies, but it *is* tied in the New Zealand Hackle style, and I've listed it here as an illustration of what can happen when you experiment.

It originated at my fly-tying bench one day some years ago. Planning to dress a Red Setter, I'd already attached a nice black squirrel-hair tail to the hook when I discovered I'd run out of hot orange chenille. During a futile search through my reserve stores of materials, I came across some fluorescent lime chenille in a box of bits and pieces, and I decided to make a Dappled Dog instead, even if it did have a black tail. I had just completed the first body segment when some yellow feathers caught my eye and, on impulse, I tied one in as the first hackle. The colour combination looked too bright and somewhat garish, so I tied in a grizzle hackle on top to subdue it a bit and, finding the result quite pleasing, I repeated the process on the second section.

The completed fly was one of those all-too-rare specimens whose general shape and proportions are perfect. Granted the cosmetics were a little unusual, but on the whole I thought it looked rather good, quite dashing in fact, and I promised myself I'd try it out on my next fishing expedition. This I did, *and* on trip after trip after that, but when the end of the season came and the fly had still not accounted for one fish or produced even a single strike, I stuck it in my cap and forgot about it.

Some years later I had a visit from Ed Volpe, an old fly-fishing friend from California. Ed wanted some trout for canning, so I took him to Lake Rotoaira which, being over-stocked and under-fished, is a place where you can confidently take a limit and keep them all with a clear conscience. But that day the trout weren't interested in the little Hamill's Killer which I'd assured him was the No. 1 fly there, and naturally after an hour's futile casting, he started looking for something else to try. The hybrid in my cap took his fancy, and despite my comments, he unhooked it and tied it on his leader. Mind you, by now the fly looked very different from what it did when first it came out of the vice. Constant wettings and exposure to the elements had caused the dye from the yellow feathers to run, staining the grizzle hackles on top and creating a faded golden-grey effect which somehow seemed to pick up a greenish tinge from the glowing lime body underneath. Casting it out, he was into a trout right away, and for the next hour he continued to take fish after fish, keeping only the very best and releasing the others while I changed flies and fumed, frustrated and fishless.

After a while his wrist got sore from playing fish, so he gave the fly back to me, and soon I was getting my share of the action while he sprawled beside me with a cold beer in his hand, a superior smile on his lips and an expression of utter contentment on his face. I don't remember how many fish we caught that day, but we came away with two of the nicest matched limits of fat rainbows you could ever wish for.

The original is still in my possession but now resides in my fly-box instead of my cap. It has contributed to the success of many subsequent fishing trips to many different places, but none has been as memorable as that special day we once had on Rotoaira using the fly on which the "dye ran" – hence the corny name.

ROTOITI KILLER (K) See KILWELL No. 2

SCOTCH POACHER (P)

Body: hot orange chenille
Tail: black squirrel tail fibres
Tinsel: oval gold
Wings: blue pukeko feathers
Hackle collar: dyed orange cock hackles

I once received a sharp reprimand from an irate Scot following a talk to an angling club during which I mentioned the Scotch Poacher. It appears that grammatically the use of the word "Scotch" is restricted to haggis and whisky (without an "e"!), so technically the proper name of this fly should be "Scots Poacher".

Regardless of how you spell it, this is a fly you'll find in almost every regular night-fisherman's collection. Many tyers like to dress it with an abnormally long tail which protrudes well beyond the end of the pukeko wing, and for some reason the smaller sizes can often be worth a try during the daytime if the water is murky or the weather overcast.

SPLIT PARTRIDGE (M)

Body: red, orange-yellow, black or green chenille
or wide silver or gold Mylar
Tail: none
Tinsel: oval silver
Wings: split partridge tail feather segments
Hackle collar: none usually

These flies are made by splitting a partridge tail feather up the central stem, spine or quill (call it whichever you like) with a very sharp blade and tying in two matching segments of it back to back as wings, secured with tinsel, Matuku style, along the top of the fly's body.

I will always have a soft spot for the Split Partridge, since I caught my very first New Zealand trout on one, but alas, the pattern does not enjoy the popularity today that it once did. This may be due in some measure to the astronomical price of partridge tail feathers, but I don't think that is the only reason. After all, its close cousin the Turkey Fly, made from turkey feathers in exactly the same style and which was once considered almost indispensable, has all but disappeared today and God knows there is no shortage of turkeys in New Zealand. No, I think it's just a question of fashions changing. If there had been something special about the split-feather wing technique, the ever-inventive Kiwi tyers would have come up with split shag, split seagull, split mynah or split muttonbird by now – with fluorescent lime-bodied versions for Taupo, of course!

TAIHAPE TICKLER (P)

Body: red chenille
Tail: small tag of red wool
Tinsel: oval silver
Wings: blue pukeko feathers
Hackle collar: dyed orange hackles

Although originally tied with a claret body and matching hackle, the Taihape Tickler is now almost exclusively dressed as shown above. When or why it changed remains a mystery. Nevertheless, it is still a first-class fish catcher and will often work when others fail.

TARAWERA KILLER (K)

See KILWELL No. 1

TAUPO TIGER (M)

Body: yellow or red
Tail: (optional) bunch dyed red hackle fibres
Tinsel: oval silver
Wings: badger cock hackles
Hackle collar: badger cock hackles

This fly used to be known as the Tiger Ross, and indeed the red-bodied version still is in some areas. I once thought the true Taupo Tiger was the yellow-bodied one and that, when tied with a red body instead, it took the name Tiger Ross, since the resultant colour combination of red, silver, black and white closely resembled that of a very popular Scottish wet fly, the Peter Ross. Old fishing books refer to both the Tiger Ross and the Tiger Ross Yellow which seems to indicate that the red version came first, but there is evidence that about fifty years ago a Hawkes Bay sportsman called James Ross may have created a fly which he named the Tiger Ross and which allegedly had a yellow body.

Keith Draper mentions this in his excellent book, *Trout Flies in New Zealand*, and goes on to explain that although Ross tried unsuccessfully to patent the pattern, he did succeed in registering the trade name, but nevertheless the fly soon appeared elsewhere under the title of Taupo Tiger. However, Keith makes no reference whatever to red being used as a body colour under either title, so as to whether red or yellow was first used, or the name Ross applied to a Scots barber or a New Zealand shopkeeper, I just don't know.

One thing I am certain of though. For some strange mysterious reason both versions under whatever name are traditionally *always* finished with red lacquered heads instead of the more customary black.

OTHER LURE STYLES

Having mastered the four preceding techniques you will now be able to tie almost all the big New Zealand lures. There are, of course, some exceptions which, while widely used, aren't tied in a style peculiar to this country. I have listed a few of them in the following section. No doubt there are others, but this isn't intended to be a dictionary of every fly ever tied in every district of every part of New Zealand.

HAIRY DOG, RED, BLACK AND GREEN (O)

Body: red, black or green chenille
Tail: bunch of black squirrel tail hair, goat hair or black FisHair
Tinsel: oval silver
Wings: same as tail
Hackle collar: same as tail

This is a grand fly for night fishing, and I can recall one fabulous session at Taupo where three of us landed almost thirty trout in the last hour of an until-then fruitless evening, all on Black Hairy Dogs. That's good fishing by any standard! Although I have seen so-called Hairy Dogs tied with yellow or orange bodies, black, red and (in some areas) green are by far the most popular.

Bind the hook shank with thread as usual and form a tail as you would for a hackle fly. Tie in chenille and oval tinsel. Wind chenille up to B to form a body; secure and trim surplus. Spiral tinsel up the body, secure and trim surplus. Tie in a small bunch of the same material as the tail *under* the hook shank at B. The tips of this bunch should not quite reach the point of the hook. Tie another slightly longer bunch on *top* of the shank at B, and this can extend to almost the same distance as the tail. Now (and this is important) *saturate* the area where these bunches are tied in with clear head cement before further binding to form the head. Whip finish and cement again. Hair is often difficult to tie in securely, and the "cement soak" at the base helps prevent it pulling out.

Fig 13

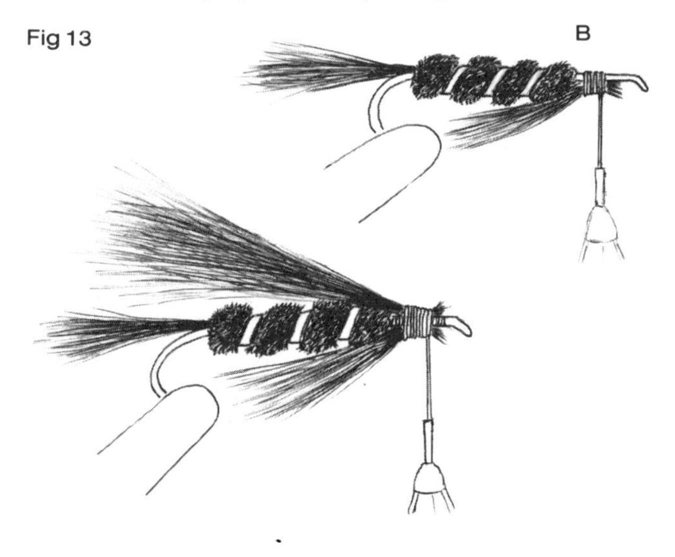

HALL'S NIGHT-TIME (O)

Body: twisted red and black chenille
Tail: (optional) bunch of grizzle hackle fibres dyed red
Wings: pair of dyed red grizzle feathers tied in at the head by the butts only
Hackle collar: (optional) from a feather dyed same as wings

The continued popularity of this fly both intrigues and amazes me, because I have yet to catch a trout with one. Furthermore, I have never seen anyone else have any success with it nor indeed do I even *know* anybody who has! Yet year after year it is requested by dealers in the Bay of Plenty area in general and Rotorua in particular. Obviously someone, somewhere, knows something I don't, but if you'd like to give it a try maybe you can find out for yourself.

Bind the hook shank with thread as always. If you want a tail (it's not essential), secure a bunch of hackle fibres as for a Matuku-style fly. Then tie in a 7.5 cm (3 in) piece of red chenille. Tie in a piece of black chenille of the same length. Now you can either wind one of them up to B, secure with thread and spiral the others over the top of it, secure and trim surplus, or you can twist the two together like a rope and wind the combination up to form a body, secure at B and trim surplus.

For the wing place two feathers back to back (as for the Matuku style) and tie in by the butts at B. Unlike a regular Matuku, however, these feathers are *not* bound to the body with tinsel. Incidentally, their length should not be much longer than the body. A hackle collar is optional, but if it's to be included, form with a third feather as you would for a Matuku-style fly. Whip finish and apply cement.

Fig 14 Hall's Night-time

HUGHIE'S MATUKU MUDDLER (O)

Body: yellow chenille
Tail: honey grizzle
Tinsel: oval gold
Hackle collar: honey grizzle
Head: deer hair
Suitable hooks: extra long shank (such as Mustad 3665A or 9672)

Tie a Parsons's Glory (or any matuku pattern you like) complete with hackle collar, but finish it two thirds of the way up the hook shank instead of at B.

Cut a pinch of deer hair and hold it, butt forward, on top of the hook shank.

1. Put one turn of thread over it and tighten. This will cause the hairs to roll around the shank. Let them.
2. Take a second turn of thread round the bunch and pull down even tighter, then a third turn, tightest of all. By now the deer hair will be flaring out every which way.
3. Push the whole affair back towards the tail as hard against the Parson's Glory part as you can, then repeat the process with another pinch of deer hair, and so on until you have filled the entire area up to B.
4. Whip finish, cut the tying thread and remove fly from the vice.
5. The deer hair you have made will at this stage look something like a well-used shaving brush or a small haystack after a gale, so with a pair of scissors give it a good haircut and trim it back until you end up with a neat symmetrical shape in proportion to the rest of the fly, either bullet-shaped or spherical is fine.
6. When trimmed to your satisfaction hold the fly upright and put a couple of generous drops of clear cement on the whip finish, letting the surplus soak down the shank into the base of the deer hair, and your fly is complete.

Claiming to be the originator of a new fly pattern is a risky business, particularly if it's a successful one. Imaginative fly tyers have been developing new patterns for countless centuries (one of the earliest on record dates back to the third century A.D.!), so by now there aren't many ideas that haven't already been tried. However, tongue-in-cheek, I'm going to lay claim as inventor of this one, but if someone else has done it earlier I apologise. In 1974 I hit upon the idea of combining the bully-like qualities of the New Zealand Parson's Glory with the buoyant deer-hair head of an American Muddler Minnow, and it was an instant success, for the first three casts I had with my new design accounted for three rainbows that totalled 20 lb (9 kg). At first I used it only for lake fishing, using large sizes with a Hi-D line in very deep water, but I later discovered that fished on a

Fig 15 How to tie a Matuku Muddler

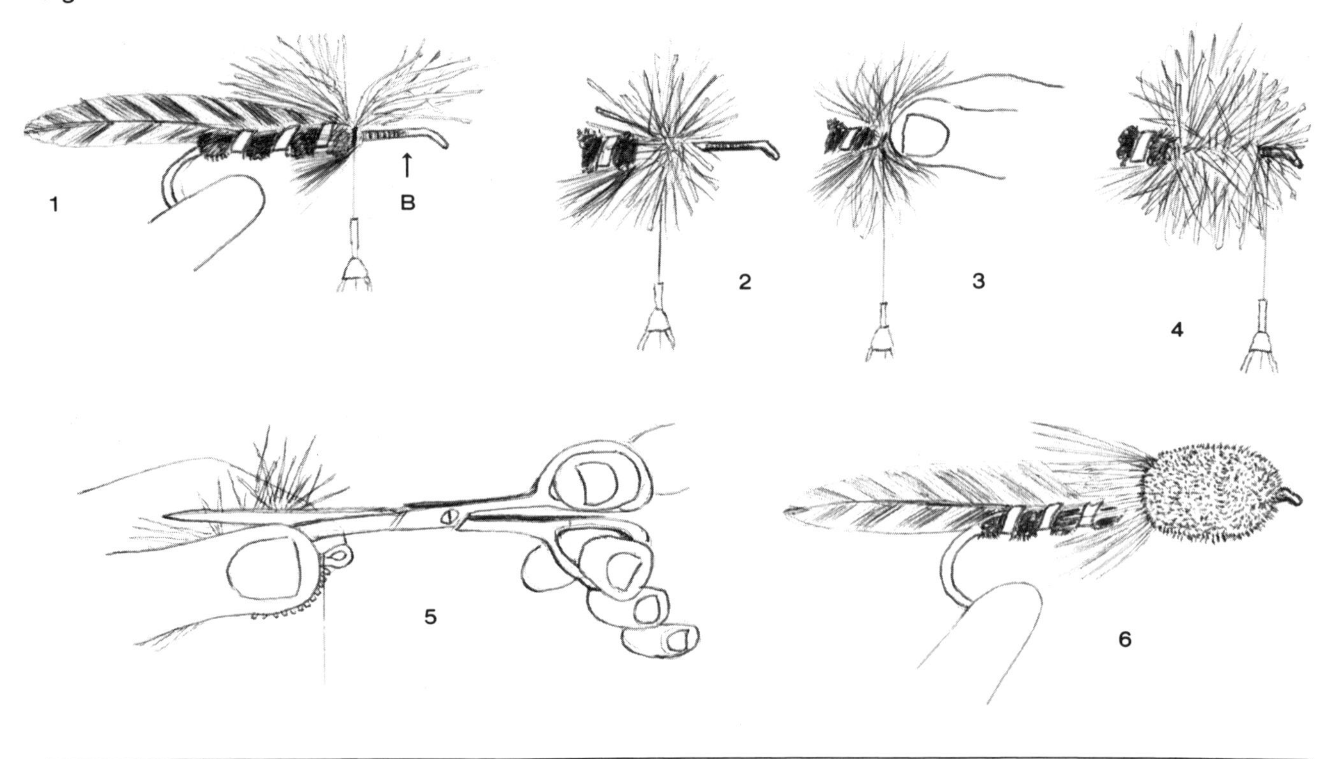

floating line across and downstream at dusk, it could be an effective lure for big river brownies. The sight of a huge bow-wave following the little wake of your Matuku Muddler across the pool is not recommended if you suffer from high blood pressure, I can assure you!

Smaller sizes liberally dressed with "Siliflote" and fished upstream as a dry fly, also work well in midsummer when trout are feeding on cicadas.

Although I have tried tying these in many combinations of feathers and body colours, I believe the original Parson's Glory theme is the most consistently effective of all.

Try a few and see for yourself, but be prepared for snide comments from fishing mates when you open your fly box: "Whatcha feed them on, cheese or birdseed?", or, when you first start casting a big one: "Bloody heck! Looks like a demented fantail!" Let them sneer, it won't be long before the next comment will be, "Er, have you got a spare one of those?"

Now a few words of advice: Since deer hair is hollow it is extremely buoyant, so if you want to fish deep water use at least a Hi-D or even a Hi-Speed Hi-D line; anything less will take forever to drag the fly anywhere near the bottom. For the same reason, if you want to fish the fly right on the bed of a river in any sort of current, you may have to use a leader of 60 cm (2 ft) or less, but I have found a normal 2.75 m (9 ft) leader is better for deep-water lake situations. There I think the line lies along the bottom while the fly floats above it, and each retrieve you make causes the fly to struggle down towards the bottom like an injured bully, rising again when you stop, so I like to make my retrieve in a series of sharp jerks, using the rod tip in conjunction with my line hand and allowing a noticeable pause in between, so that my "injured baitfish" rests between efforts to gain the safety of the lake bed again. Of course, nobody really knows what goes on down there or what the trout makes of it all, but whatever it is I can honestly say that some of the takes I have had with the Matuku Muddler have been among the most violent and savage I have ever experienced. When fishing "over the lip" from an anchored boat, I have often had the whole top half of the rod jerked under the water when a big fish struck, so I don't mess around with dainty 6 or 7 lb tippets any more! Besides, the strain of casting one of the big, bulky, wind-resistant flies requires nylon of some substance, as well as a rod with a bit of backbone. Indeed, if there happens to be a breeze in your face, casting one at all can be a tricky business, and I suggest you try and remember to keep your backcast high and your head low in such situations!

NYMPHS, WET FLIES AND DRY FLIES

Most of the big "flies" you've now mastered represent small baitfish or koura rather than actual flies. But trout like to eat other things, too. Whether, like us, they get bored with the same old "meat and two veg" on the menu every day and look for a change of diet or instinctively they seek missing vitamins or other substances that insects provide I don't know, but the fact remains that trout eat insects, and quite a lot of them at that. Even in places where there is always an abundance of food like bullies, smelt and crayfish, trout will sometimes ignore all and go for a feeding spree on green manuka beetles blown onto the water from bankside vegetation, while we've all heard of the famous "evening rise" when the trout forsake their daytime hiding places to come up and gorge on tiny mayflies floating on the surface. Anglers discovered the trout's penchant for insects a very long time ago and have, in fact, been successfully using artificial flies to catch them for over 1700 years! There is a very accurate description of this in a book called *De Natura Animalium* written by one Aelian in the third century A.D. Since they only brought books out in singles in those days, it is unlikely you'll find it in your local library, but here is a quote from the relevant chapter entitled (approximately) "Unusual fishing in Macedonia":

> There is a river called Astraeus flowing midway between Berea and Thessalonica, in which are produced certain spotted fish whose food

consists of insects which fly about the river. These insects are dissimilar to all other kinds found elsewhere; they are not like wasps, nor would one naturally compare them with the flies called ephemera, nor do they resemble bees. But they are as impudent as flies, as large as the Ant Hedon, of the same colour as wasps and they buzz like bees. The natives call this insect the "Hippurus".

As these flies float on the top of the water in pursuit of food, they attract the notice of the fish, which swim upon them. When the fish spies one of these insects on the top of the water, it swims quietly underneath it, taking care not to agitate the surface, lest it should scare away the prey; so approaching it, as it were, under the shadow it opens its mouth and gulps it down, just as a wolf seizes a sheep, or an eagle a goose, and having done this it swims away beneath the ripple.

The fishermen are aware of all this; but they do not use these flies for bait because handling would destroy their natural colour, injure the wings and spoil them as a lure. On this account the natural insect is in ill repute with the fishermen, who cannot make use of it. They manage to circumvent the fish, however, by the following clever piscatorial device. They cover a hook with red wool, and upon this they fasten two feathers of a waxy appearance which grow under a cock's wattle, they have a reed six feet long and a fishing line about the same length; they drop this lure upon the water and the fish being attracted by the colour becomes extremely excited, proceeds to meet it, anticipating from its beautiful appearance a most delicious repast; but, as with extended mouth it seizes the lure, it is held fast by the hook, and being captured, meets with a very sorry entertainment.

Fascinating, isn't it? Now I expect you'd like to try your hand at tying some of these small insect imitations. There are two types, those that float and those that don't. Let me explain why because, though I don't want to give you a lecture on entomology, I feel if you understand a little about *what* you are trying to imitate you will make a better job of tying it, while knowing something about the behaviour pattern of the originals makes the choice of the correct fly simpler at the waterside *and* can improve the way you fish it, too!

Many waterside insects such as mayflies, stoneflies, caddis flies, dragonflies, damselflies and so on hatch from eggs laid under water and actually spend most of their lives as sub-aquatic creatures before coming to the surface, splitting their skins and emerging as adult insects, a process known as metamorphosis. During this pre-adult period they are known collectively as "nymphs" or, in the case of caddis flies, "larvae". Trout are exceedingly fond of both, eagerly seeking out and devouring them in great quantities and in some areas this amounts to 75–80 per cent of their entire food intake. Little wonder that an artificial nymph cast upstream and allowed to tumble back over the riverbed towards the angler can often be such an effective way of taking a hungry trout.

One of the more important varieties of these insects from the angler's point of view is the mayfly, and it is interesting to learn a little about its lifestyle.

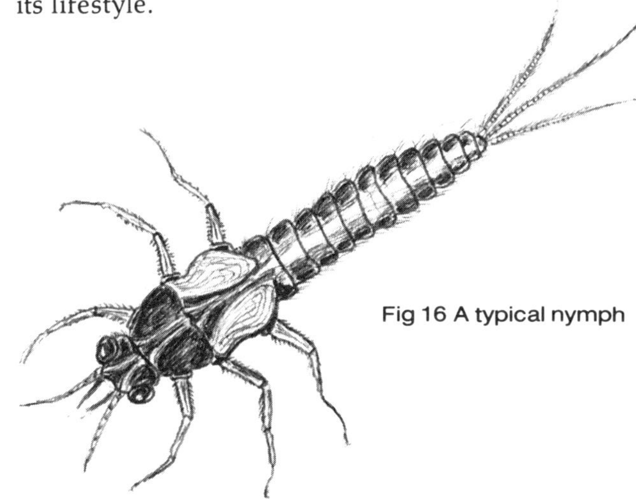

Fig 16 A typical nymph

MAYFLIES

After a period of time all nymphs reach a point, usually in the evening, where the urge to escape from their watery environment becomes too strong to resist and they make their way out of the water, some species crawling up rocks or reeds and others like the mayflies actively rising to the surface. This mass-migration period attracts the attention of the ever-hungry trout and usually prompts active feeding, which can develop into a near frenzy when those nymphs which swim up to the top start struggling out of their skins. (Imagine how easy it would be to capture a person in the process of getting out of a wetsuit!) Therefore, the observant angler often uses a small wet fly fished just under the surface to simulate this emerging situation.

Those nymphs fortunate enough to avoid being eaten before escaping from their nymphal shucks emerge on the surface, floating for a moment on the water while they dry out enough to fly away and, during this brief period, once again they are

Fig 17 Mayfly

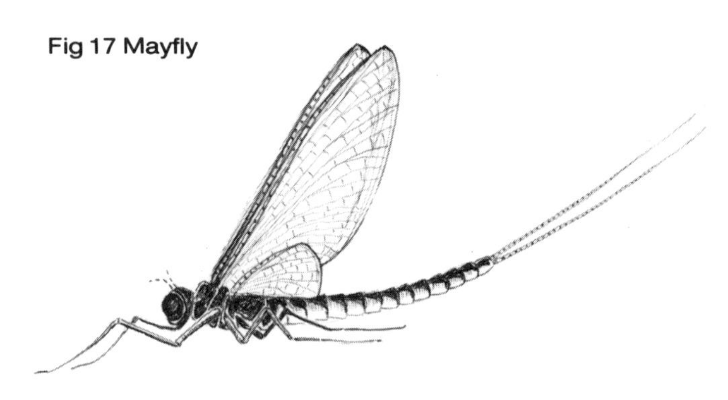

liable to be ambushed from beneath and dragged under by the ever-watchful, ever-hungry trout. The surviving "duns", as they are called, fly off into the dusk and settle safely in the sheltering foliage of the bankside vegetation, emerging again the following evening for a nuptial mating flight. Often they have changed colour over the previous 24 hours and in this second appearance they are known as "spinners". During their brief sojourn in the air they do not eat; they don't have to because after mating, both sexes die and their floating spent bodies once again become food for the trout – usually at first light the following morning. Various shapes and colours of dry flies are used to imitate all these "floating" periods of the mayfly's short adult life, first as duns, then as spinners and finally as spent spinners.

I once saw an amusing cartoon in which a little man complete with white robe, harp and halo kneels on a cloud before an angel with a clipboard. "Ah yes," says the angel, "here we are. You are being reincarnated and sent back to Earth as a mayfly. Have a nice day!" Now that you know a little about the life of the mayfly, you too can appreciate the joke.

Mayflies come in all sizes and colours from pale olives and sulphurs through smoky greys and browns to dark charcoal or claret tones, and while in the nymphal stage, range from muddy greys to bright amber shades.

Another very important and extremely interesting insect which it will certainly pay you to know about is the caddis fly.

CADDIS FLIES

Have you ever stayed on fishing well after dark because there was a good rise in the river and the trout were going mad, but you couldn't catch one? Pausing to change flies for the umpteenth time you switch on your flashlight and within seconds you are surrounded by thousands of little fawnish moth-like insects that scuttle all over your hands, crawl into your ears and get up your nose? No, they aren't moths like everybody says, they're caddis flies. I've come across them in every piece of trout water I've ever fished anywhere in the world, and everywhere trout love them. They

Fig 18 Caddis fly

gorge themselves until their stomachs are stuffed as tightly packed as luncheon sausage and, in fact, I would go so far as to say that trout would possibly prefer caddis over any other insect. Whole books have been written about them and believe me, if you can tie good imitations of all stages of the caddis fly's progess, figure out which one to use, in which size and in which colour – and fish it properly – you've got trout fishing licked.

The caddis fly lays her eggs on, or just under, the surface of the water. They sink to the bottom among the gravel or general debris and eventually each hatches into a small grub-like larva. Being relatively helpless most species – but not all – immediately set about building themselves a kind of individual protective mobile home, each using sand, gravel, small twigs, bits of straw or vegetable matter to construct a little one-ended tube which the owner can drag around as it searches for food or quickly withdraw into if danger approaches. (See fig. 19.) If the approaching danger happens to be a trout, this manoeuvre is usually of little help to the caddis larva because the trout will eat it, house and all, which is one of the reasons that when cleaning a trout you will sometimes find the stomach packed with debris. That's all that remains of the unfortunate caddis larvae's houses, the owners having been digestible and their castles not!

Fig 19 Caddis larva

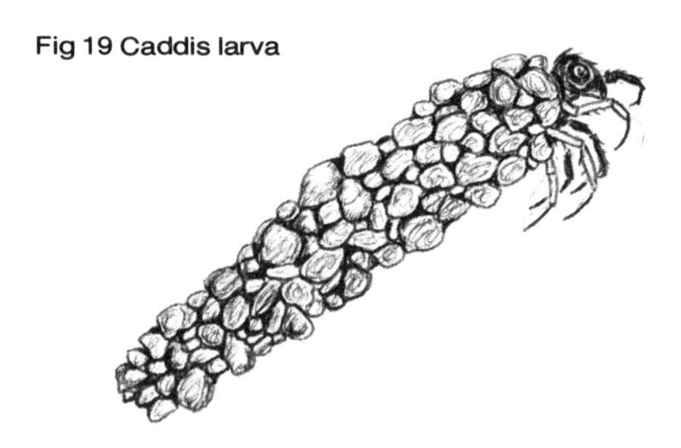

After a period of time under water most species of the surviving caddis larvae withdraw into their little fortresses, seal up the doors and retire for a

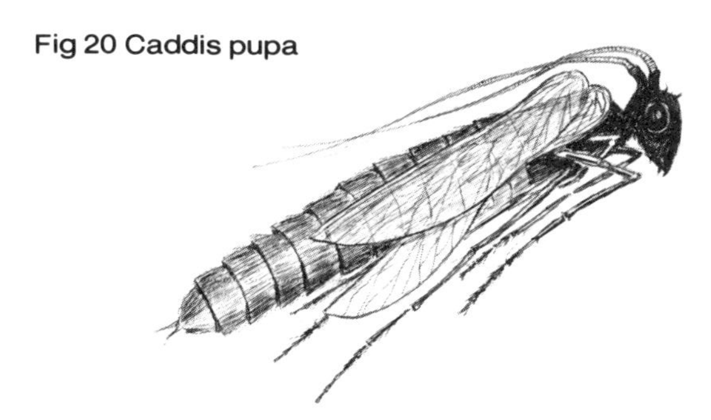
Fig 20 Caddis pupa

few weeks, during which time a metamorphosis takes place. The larva changes into a pupa, (see fig. 20), a semi-insect with long trailing legs and half-developed wings which, most likely late on a summer's evening, re-opens the hideaway and crawls out. During the change from larva to pupa, a mass of tiny gas bubbles have formed around the newly acquired limbs and these act as little buoyant balloons, which whisk the owner to the surface in double-quick time. On arrival there a second metamorphosis takes place. The pupa bursts its skin, the adult insect crawls out and scuttles off over the surface of the water.

So once again we have anglers using larval imitations on the bottom, wet flies to represent the rising or emerging pupae just under the surface or dry flies that hopefully look like floating adult insects. Simple, eh? Except that you may arrive at the river after work, and there in the fast fading light you find the air full of flies and fish rising everywhere. There are perhaps five types of mayfly and two species of caddis on the water, all of different sizes and colours and all seemingly metamorphosing at once. Are the trout taking everything edible, rising nymphs and pupae, emergers and adult insects, mayflies and caddis alike? Or are they being selective and only taking one, and if so, which one? Frantically you change fly after fly until it's too dark to see and then, after a fishless evening, you bump into old Fred on the way home in the dark. He's had a limit, including a 6-lb brownie you'd give your eye teeth for. What fly? Oh, they weren't taking anything coming off the water, they were taking big dark adult female caddis flies that were coming out of the bushes and laying their eggs on the water, didn't you see them? You know, the ones with the green egg sac. He spotted them right off, he did. Thought you would have, too . . . . Yes, very humiliating that sort of thing can be, but next time it may be old Fred who "couldn't seem to get on to them at all tonight" and who pretends not to notice the 8-lb rainbow you carry so casually. Such is the stuff angling is made of!

Incidentally, the origin of the name "caddis fly" is an interesting one. In medieval times when department stores were not as widespread as they are today, people bought a lot of merchandise from peddlers who travelled from town to town selling their various wares. A right promiscuous bunch they were, too, if we are to believe all that has been written about them, which is probably the reason for the reputation honest travelling salesmen have to this day! Anyway, the ones who sold cloth were known as "caddice men", and to advertise the fact they sewed swatches of different cloth all over their clothes until they were literally encased in samples. The larvae of the caddis fly in their little cases of pebbles and sticks must have reminded some early entomologist of the caddice men, and so the name evolved. Another popular name given by the English to this fly is "sedge", so if you ever see a pattern for a "sedge fly" you will know it was originally tied as a caddis imitation.

Don't think that trout confine themselves to taking aquatic insects from the surface in the evenings though. Many types of land-based insects meet a sudden end in a trout's jaws during the daytime after they accidentally fall on the water, or even fly close enough to the surface to catch the trout's ever-watchful eye. These terrestrials include bees, wasps, grasshoppers, ants, cicadas and crickets as well as the green beetles mentioned earlier, and thus you can see that dry flies are used to represent a very wide variety of surface food.

So there we have it. Artificial *nymphs* to imitate

the sub-aquatic stages of waterside insects' life cycles, little *wet flies* to represent their emergence as adults and *dry flies* to suggest all kinds of floating trout-food.

But before I go on, a word of warning. This is only a very basic layout of an extremely complex subject, and in one's thirst for knowledge it is all too easy to get so absorbed in the different orders and genera of myriads of insects which form part of the trout's diet, not to mention the Latin names for them, that one frequently forgets the object of the exercise was simply to help choose a fly that will fool a fish.

The poet Alexander Pope said, "A little learning is a dangerous thing", and this was never truer than when applied to entomology.

Now I agree that a rudimentary knowledge of the size, colour and behaviour pattern of the creatures that comprise a trout's diet is a good thing. After all, there's little point in offering a big koura imitation on a sunken line when the trout are hell-bent on exterminating the mayfly population on the surface, is there? But there are literally thousands of different insects and to try and learn everything there is to know about all of them would require a lifetime of intensive study with very little time left for fishing. In any case, as I have repeatedly stressed throughout this book, it's impossible to tie an exact imitation anyway, so my approach to what fly to use is to try and identify what the trout are feeding on, based either on observation or experience. For example, if trout are rising during the day in the summertime I look for an obvious "hatch" of mayflies, and if there is one, what size and colour are they? Small, medium or large? Black, cream, grey or ginger? Then I try to find something similar in my fly box. If there *isn't* anything obvious on the water, I'll try an Adams or perhaps a small Coch-y-bondhu or other green beetle imitation since few trout will ignore such a tasty morsel on a warm summer's day. If that doesn't work, I'll change to a brace of drab little wets, twitching them enticingly under the surface like emerging nymphs struggling free from their skins as they are swept helplessly downstream, just in case that's what the trout are really feeding on. All I'm trying to do is present something that resembles approximately in size, shape, colour and behaviour what the trout is likely to be interested in eating, and I really don't care what the Latin name for it is.

I remember once accompanying two learned American fly fishermen on a trip up the Rangitaiki. They were both very deeply "into" entomology, and when we arrived at the river there was a great rise going on, but to my surprise they appeared to be in no rush to get started. Instead they captured a sample of an emerging dun and with the aid of a hand-held magnifying glass and a copy of *Art Flick's Streamside Guide* they fell to arguing over proper identification of the insect and the proper imitation to use. One held that it was a member of the Isonychia group of the Ephemerella family and therefore necessitated a Lead Wing Coachman as the proper imitation, while the other poohooed the idea, pointing out that Isonychia nymphs only metamorphosed in the late evening. The proper identification, he said, was *Ephemerella invaria* or at least an Antipodean version of it and as such could only be duplicated by a Dark Hendrickson. The argument got hot and heavy and went on until I could wait no longer: a daytime rise like this doesn't happen every day, and when it does you have to make the most of it, so, knotting on a fly of similar size and colour to the natural, I presented it to the nearest rising fish. I was into a beautiful 3-lb rainbow right away, and the scream of the reel brought the two running breathlessly to my side, still clutching magnifying glasses and reference book. "Which fly did you use?" they asked, as I netted the trout, unhooked and released it, "Hendrickson or Lead Wing Coachman?" As a general rule I'm a fairly easygoing type, but I was rapidly losing my temper. Here were two guys who'd travelled 10,000 kilometres to go fishing. I'd taken time off to bring them up to share one of my favourite pieces of water, the trout were rising like crazy and all they could do was argue about exact imitations and proper Latin terminology! I couldn't resist it, I shouldn't have done it, but I did. The temptation was too great. Looking at them earnestly and with as straight a face as I could muster, I said, "Gentlemen, I should have thought it was obvious, but as strangers I suppose you can be forgiven. Up here I use only two flies, the WGJ and the BBB."

"Really?" came the astonished reply. "Those are new patterns to us. What are they, Ephemeroptera or Plecoptera?"

"I'm not sure," I said, gravely. "The WGJ is a wee ginger job, and the BBB a big black bastard, and as far as I'm concerned, that's all you need on this river!"

In the end each of them fished with his own particular "exact imitation", and both caught plenty of fish before the rise finished, but they were still arguing over the proper Latin orders as we drove back home. I felt a bit guilty, because actually I lied. Sometimes I use a BGJ and a WBB as well . . . .

Then there were Gary and Fred, two great fishing mates of mine who had really got heavily involved with entomology and "matching the hatch". We'd drive to this particular chalk stream where you could see fish rising right beside where we parked the car, but, muttering something about a "false rise", my friends would ignore all this action and potter about with little nets and jars, catching nymphs and trying to identify them, taking air and water temperatures, checking the barometric pressure, pH factor of the water and God knows what else besides. Then they'd pore over reference books for half an hour before triumphantly announcing that a hatch of some particular fly would occur between 10.30 and 11.00 a.m. and only then would they put up their rods, attach the approved "exact imitation" and confidently await the predicted rise.

While all this was going on I'd be catching fish using a little partridge-hackled Hughie's Bug and a scruffy nondescript wet fly on the dropper. The boys would study these in amazement and give me 100 reasons why they *shouldn't* be working this time of day, but instead of accepting my proffered fly box and getting into the action, they'd sit and wait for the "main rise" coming on. Frequently it didn't, and then it was back to the nets and jars and thermometers and reference books for another prediction. I kid you not, I have seen those two mess about like this all day without wetting a line until the ever-dependable evening rise took place! Can you imagine driving *5 hours* just for one hour's fishing?

Yet both these stories are true. I haven't told them just to prove my superiority as a fisherman for, Lord knows, I've had my share of blank days too, I can assure you! No, I'm simply pointing out how easy it is to get so wrapped up in the study of entomology that you can forget the object of the exercise in the first place was to tie a fly that will catch fish. By all means learn the difference between mayflies and caddis flies and dragonflies, get to know what their nymphs look like, how they behave and what sort of conditions they like, then try tying approximate representations and *fish them* with confidence. After all, there isn't much percentage in having a box full of "exact" imitations, knowing all their Latin names off by heart and then letting them stay in there, is there?

Many years ago I was fishing a loch with an old ghillie near Inverness in the Scottish Highlands. In those days I rather fancied myself as a pretty sharp caster, and I'm afraid I was trying to impress him with my ability to aerialise 20 metres or so of line while he "stroked the water" with a team of wee wet flies, casting a short line among the ripples just ahead of our drifting boat. When he'd landed his tenth trout, and I'd had only one miserable tiddler, I muttered something about it being his lucky day. The old man laid down his rod, lit his pipe and, gazing out over the grey misty lake, said 'Och, it's the fine caster you are, laddie, but ye'll no catch fush iff yer flee's no in the watter." I never forgot that lesson. Incidentally, old Alistair only ever used three flies the whole time I knew him, a Peter Ross, a Mallard and Claret and a moth-eaten ragged thing that might once have been a Greenwell's Glory, and with these he usually caught more trout than anyone else. Maybe there is a lesson there, too, somewhere!

But I'm digressing.

Let's have a go at tying some basic patterns of each. You have already got all the tools you'll need, but there are a few additional materials which will come in handy and which we'll discuss in the next chapter.

MATERIALS

HOOKS

Hooks come in a mind-blowing, bewildering variety of types and shapes. There are hooks of both heavy and light wire, with shanks that are long or short, eyes that turn up or down, points that are straight or offset and shapes that curve in a semi-circle or bend at 90°. They can be bronzed or japanned in finish or plated with tin, nickel, cadmium or even gold. Each has its own particular devotee, so little wonder the beginner is confused and unsure of what to choose.

Having used them all at one time or another, I've settled on Mustad 9672 for most of my wets, dries and nymphs. These are what is known as "3x long" which simply means the shanks are the same length as shanks of standard hooks 3 sizes larger. I find this tiny extra margin invaluable by providing just that little bit more space in which to add an extra hackle, or perhaps slightly more lead – when required in a nymph, for example. However, since they aren't available any smaller than No. 16, it also means I am restricted to tying flies whose proportions are no smaller than a normal No. 10 or perhaps No. 12 artificial. This should not create any problems for the reader; after all, this book is designed for "ten-thumbed beginners", and believe me, when you start tying these relatively small flies for the first time you'll really appreciate all the space you can get! Later, if you want to graduate to *really* tiny patterns, by all means experiment with whatever alternatives are available, but in the meantime I suggest you begin with 9672 (see fig 3b, page 16).

THREAD

Although black Monocord is probably the most useful, many insect-type artificials are best tied with lighter colours. Buy some in yellow, insect green and silver grey.

LEAD WIRE

Because they are often fished right down on the river bed, a lot of nymphs benefit greatly by the addition of some lead to the hook-shank before construction of the lure commences. Fine lead wire is available packaged expressly for the purpose, but you can sometimes find bulk spools of fine solder in radio repair shops and although this tends to be a somewhat expensive investment initially, the cost per centimetre is much less than buying it in small lots. Some sports shops sell lead-core trolling line by the metre, and 10 metres of this, stripped of its protective braided sheath, will provide enough lead to tie dozens of nymphs. If you are of an extremely frugal nature, you can save such things as old toothpaste tubes and the lead foil that covers the corks on some wine bottles. Opened out and rolled flat they can be cut into narrow strips and wound round the hook to provide the required weight.

Here are two "don'ts" to remember when using lead.

Don't use too much. Overweighted nymphs are both difficult and dangerous to cast. The correct amount shouldn't need to exceed 8 cm at the very most.

Don't tie weighted nymphs on a hook bigger than No. 10. It's illegal in most of the country!

PEACOCK HERL

This is a superb material for making the bodies in many different patterns of flies and nymphs. It's cheap, so buy plenty. You're unlikely ever to have too much.

BROWN PARTRIDGE FEATHERS

These fragile little speckled feathers make great legs for nymphs and wet flies. Unfortunately, they are becoming increasingly hard to find and correspondingly expensive, but a little goes a long way, so if you see them, buy them!

COCK PHEASANT TAIL FEATHERS

Fibres from these are used for tails on a good many wets, dries and nymphs.

FURS

Bodies made of fur have a desirable lustre and translucence obtainable with few other materials. Dyed seal's fur in red, yellow, green, olive, orange, claret, black and brown is useful at one time or another, as are the many different shades of natural fur from such common animals as possums, rabbits and hares. Furs from the European mole and the North American muskrat also have their uses.

FINE COPPER WIRE

This is usually sold in small coils or spools, but an electrician friend may be able to provide an old armature (for next to nothing) which will provide enough wire to last you a lifetime. Used mainly for ribbing or as extra security for relatively fragile body materials like herl or fur, fine wire can also be utilised as an underbody to provide a little extra weight necessary for some small nymph patterns where lead is too bulky to use.

PRIMARY WING FEATHERS

Slips cut out from the big primary and secondary wing feathers of mallard ducks are used for winging both wet and dry flies as well as for wing-cases on many nymphs. Primaries from the blackbird or starling are also good for the same purpose on smaller-sized patterns.

LATEX RUBBER

Strips cut from old bicycle tubes or discarded

domestic protective rubber gloves can be used for creating some interesting bodies on nymph and pupae imitations or as nymphal wing-cases in lieu of feather slips. Cream, brown and black are probably the most desirable.

TINSEL

While the medium or large oval tinsel you've already got for tying the big lures *can* be pressed into service, a spool of FINE is better for the small flies. It's cheap enough, so get both silver and gold. You can experiment with "embossed" or other types if you like, but the oval is quite satisfactory and much stronger.

TEAL FEATHERS

Many old wet-fly patterns call for wings of black and white barred teal plumage which is very difficult to obtain these days. Similar feathers can be obtained from a paradise duck (which incidentally isn't really a duck but a goose), and you can sometimes come across a mallard drake with darker than usual flank feathers, but frankly unless you happen to find some or particularly want to tie some pattern that calls for a teal wing, I wouldn't worry about them. This also applies to another old-fashioned favourite, bronze mallard.

FLOSS

Several patterns of dries, wets and nymphs require floss for the bodies. Originally of silk which often changed colour dramatically when wet, floss today is usually synthetic and doesn't necessarily produce the same effect. You can buy a little box of a dozen assorted colours which will last for a long time.

WAX

Although *all* flies used to be tied with waxed thread, to be honest I don't bother with it for general fly tying, but for making dubbed fur bodies it is almost indispensable. I have tried all kinds, and the best I have found, bar none, is a brand called "Overton's Wonder Wax" which comes in a dispenser rather like a shaving soap stick. If you can find some, buy it.

GOLDEN PHEASANT TIPPETS

A few of the golden, black-tipped fibres from a golden pheasant's neck feathers feature as tails on a great many wet flies. I have substituted fibres from much cheaper cock pheasant's tail feathers and haven't found any loss of efficiency as a result!

COCK HACKLES

The relatively cheap hackle used in the construction of big lures is fine for wet flies and nymphs. In fact, it is better since the soft webby texture of the fibres soaks up water like a sponge, and they wriggle enticingly under water like the legs of a struggling aquatic creature, but when you come to tie dry flies, it's an entirely different matter. You see, a good traditional dry fly must float, poised like a ballerina on her toes, supported by the tips of the hackle fibres (and possibly the tail if the pattern calls for one), and the only feathers that provide the stiff springy hackles required to do this come from well-matured roosters. Now a cockerel eats as much as a hen, doesn't provide eggs and gets as tough as an old boot once the bloom of youth starts to fade, so few commercial poultry breeders raise old roosters — there's no profit in it. The few that do have to put a fair investment into having and feeding the quarrelsome semi-exotic birds necessary to produce the colours and patterns of wiry feathers demanded by dry-fly tyers, and therefore the cost of the capes eventually offered for sale is relatively high. I say "relatively high" because you do in fact get a great many feathers from one cape, but you will have to pay about five to six times the price of a regular neck for even a mediocre one with feathers good enough for a dry fly, and sometimes as much as 50 times more for the absolute best.

Fig 21 Where cock hackles come from

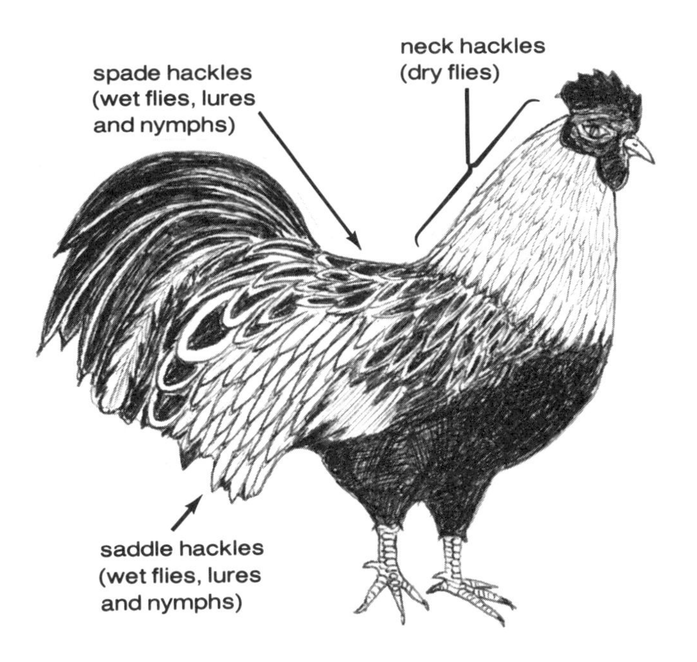

But remember, it takes just as much time and effort to tie a dry fly with cheap, rubbishy hackles as it does with good-quality ones, and since the fly with the cheap hackle won't float for toffee when it is finished anyway, what is the point of the exercise? At the time of writing (1982) a cheap neck or cape is about $2 or $3, a reasonable dry-fly quality cape perhaps $15, and a top-grade one up to $100. Believe me, you're better off investing $45 in three decent ones than in 15 assorted cheapies. The old adage that you can't make a silk purse out of a sow's ear was never truer than when it comes to making good dry flies. So buy the very best you can afford and protect them with lots of mothballs – moth grubs always seem to enjoy devouring the best ones first!

How does one tell a good cape from a poor one – aside from the price tag? Well, experience is definitely the best teacher, but here are a few points to watch for. Top-quality feathers are springy, long and slender, with the length of the hackle fibres being nearly equal for the entire length of the feather. They have a rich shiny gloss which extends for most of the top surface, as does the colour and the pattern. Cheaper-grade feathers are usually much more tapered, lack this brilliant sheen and frequently go pale or whitish halfway down their stems, while the reverse sides often have a chalky appearance absent in quality ones. The hackle fibres of good dry-fly feathers are stiff and wiry in comparison to the relatively limp ones found on ordinary feathers, too. But really, to begin with anyway, I recommend you put your trust in a knowledgeable tackle dealer who carries a good stock of quality materials and preferably who ties dry flies himself. If there isn't one in your area, you'll have to go by price alone. Mind you, don't turn up your nose at the offer of the skin from an old rooster.

Here is a list of the most desirable feather patterns and colours. Obviously you won't be able to acquire all of them at once, but if you are going to tie a lot of the more popular dry flies, all will be required at one time or another.

BLACK, BLUE DUN	Since neither of these occur very often in nature they will probably be dyed.
GRIZZLE	Really good quality ones are *extremely* expensive. They will always have very definitely defined black and white alternating bars.
HONEY GRIZZLE, GINGER, NATURAL BROWN, RED OR CREAM	These come in an infinite variety of shades, so when I come across a particularly successful one I try to buy another like it while I still have the original as a sample.
FURNACE	Regular furnace is a reddish-ginger with a bold black stripe up the centre. If you ever come across one with black-*tipped* hackle fibres as well, grab it! It's a

genuine coch-y-bondhu which is very highly sought-after and as rare as hens' teeth.

BADGER

This is quite a common feather which enjoys good sales and yet for the life of me I cannot think of a single popular dry-fly pattern which calls for it! At a pinch it can be substituted for the very much more expensive grizzle.

NYMPHS

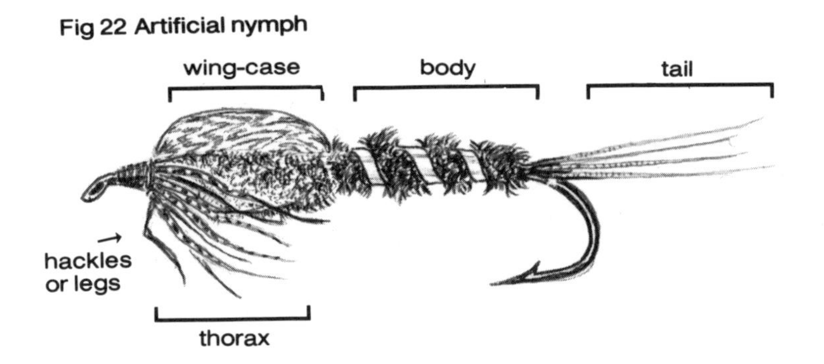

Fig 22 Artificial nymph

Let's try tying a relatively simple nymph. This one isn't any particular pattern, but it will incorporate the use of a few of the new materials you've acquired, show you some new techniques and catch plenty of trout, too, even if your first attempts don't come out exactly perfect.

Here's what you'll need:

Mustad 9672 size 12 hook
Hare's fur
Fine oval tinsel or fine copper wire
Peacock herl
Cock pheasant tail feather
A mallard primary wing feather or
strip of black latex rubber
A small cheap-quality ginger feather
Fine lead wire
Clear body-cement
Yellow Monocord

1. Secure hook in vice.
2. Bind shank from B to A.
3. Tie in 3 or 4 cock pheasant tail fibres. As this is a general, all-purpose nymph the length of the tail can vary. I prefer the tail to be as long

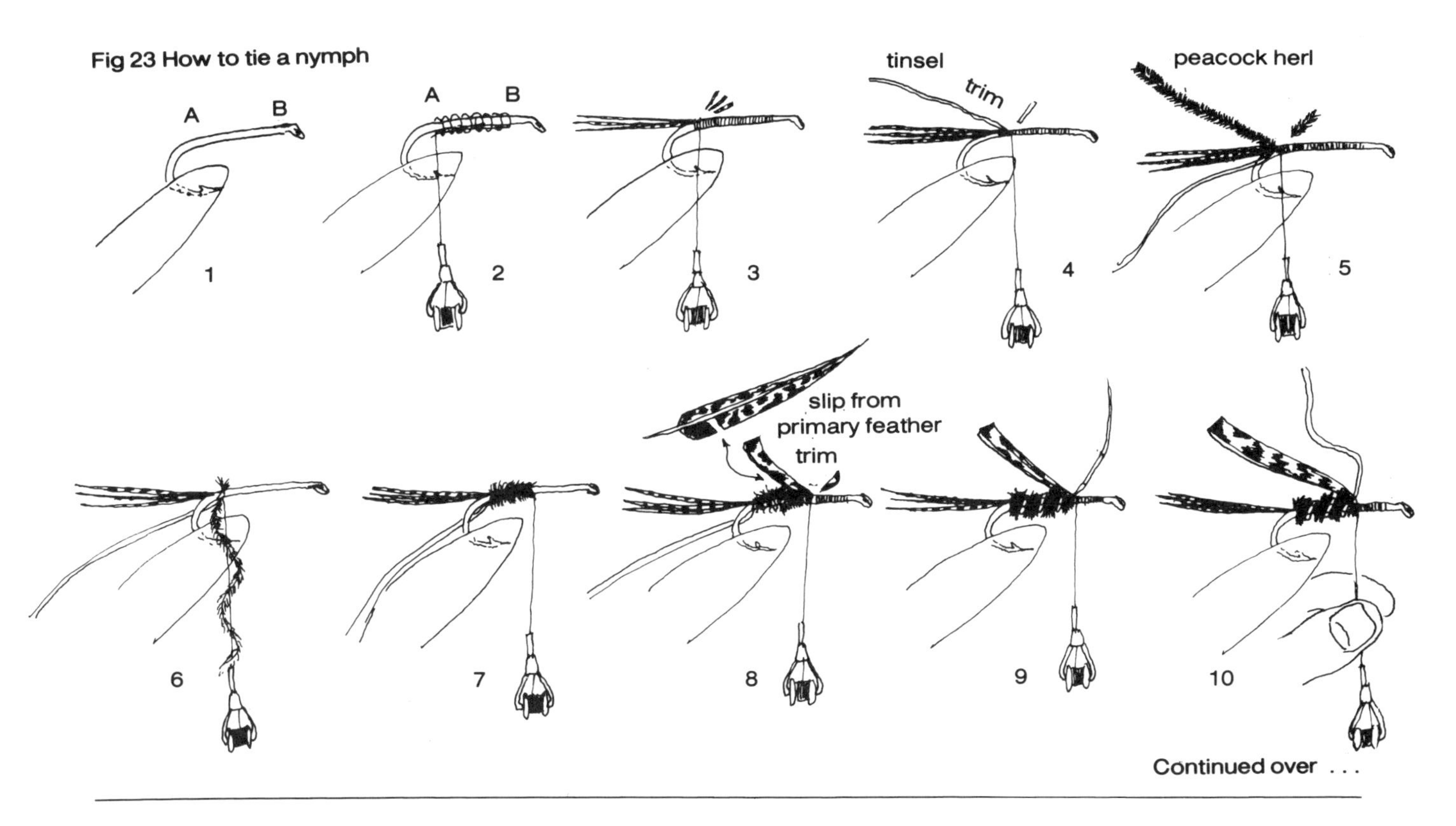

Fig 23 How to tie a nymph

Continued over . . .

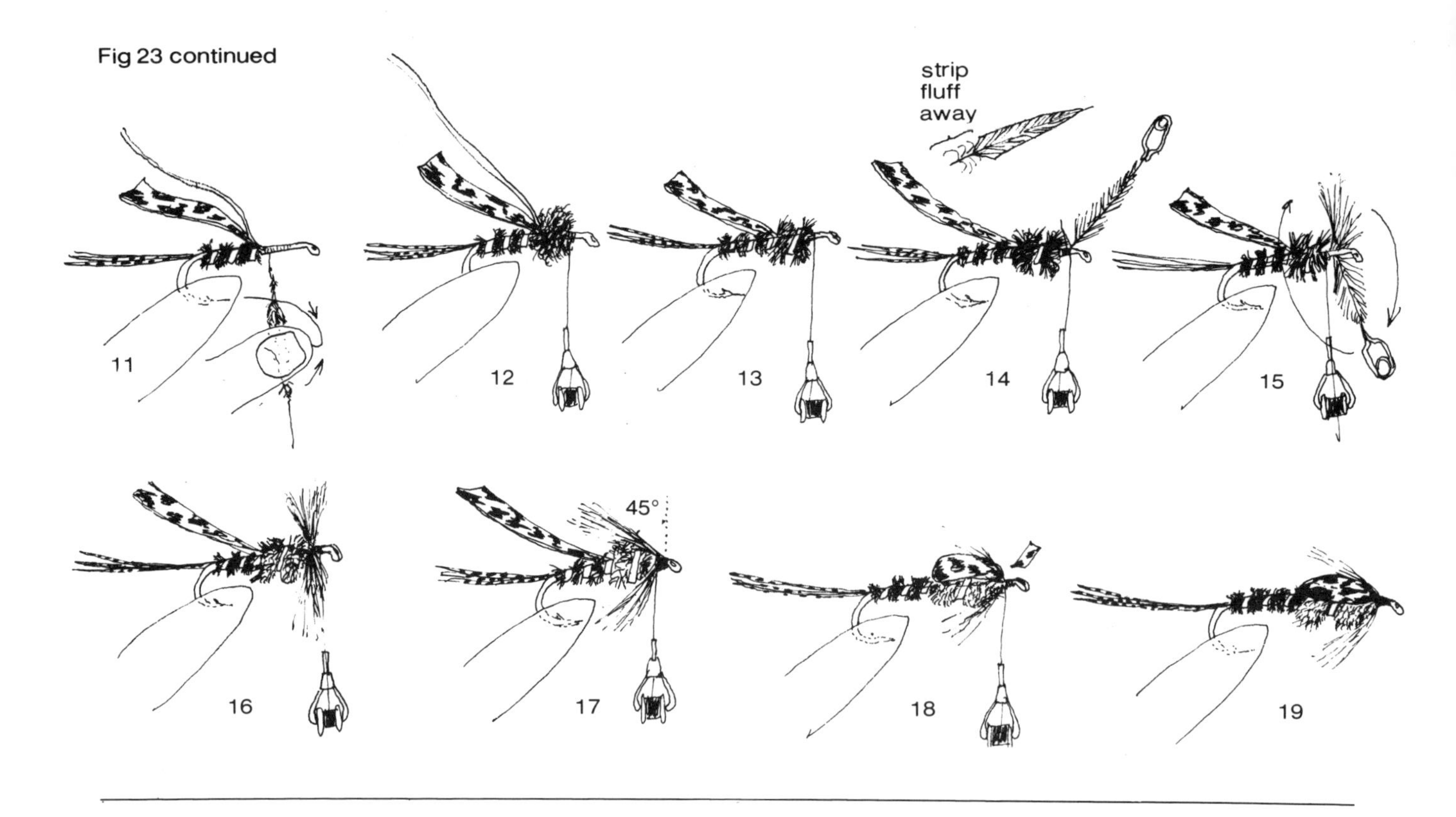
Fig 23 continued
strip
fluff
away
11
12
13
14
15
16
45°
17
18
19

as the body, but anywhere between that and half a body length is OK.

4. Tie in 5 cm (2 in) oval tinsel or copper wire.
5. Tie in 1 or 2 strands or peacock herl. If a weighted nymph is not required, go on to (6). If the nymph *is* to be weighted, wind thread halfway up the shank, tie in lead wire. The amount you use may vary according to its thickness and the weight you require, but regard 8 mm as the maximum. Bind it back down to A along the top of the shank, then wind the lead three quarters of the way up the shank and back down over itself 3 or 4 turns. Make sure each turn of lead wire is firm and close to its neighbour. Wind thread up and down the lead wire in a criss-cross fashion until it is really firmly held, and finish up at A. Drench lead with clear body-cement (see fig. 24).
6. Draw 8 cm or so of the thread through the wax, then wind the peacock herl around it, thus forming a sort of rope.
7. Wind this herl "rope" about halfway up shank and tie in and trim surplus.
8. Cut a slip about 2 mm wide from a primary wing feather or a strip of dark latex, tie in and trim surplus.
9. Spiral tinsel or copper wire over herl and tie in, but *don't* trim.
10. Now we come to a new technique called *dubbing*. Here we're using hare's fur but the technique is used for all hair and fur bodies. Wax another 8 cm of thread and squeeze a pinch of fur to the tacky surface (see fig 25, step 1).
11. Roll between your fingers until you have formed a sort of cigar-shaped furry rope (see fig. 25, step 2).
12. Wind this around shank to create a furry lump. This will be the thorax of the fly.
13. Spiral a couple of turns of the tinsel or copper wire over it to secure, tie in and trim surplus.
14. Strip fluff from base of feather and tie in the stem.

15. Wind feather 2 or 3 times around shank.
16. Tie down and trim off remainder of tip.
17. Wind thread back towards tail until hackle fibres are held back at about 45°.
18. Bring the feather slip or latex strip over the top of the thorax and tie securely in and trim surplus away. This represents the natural nymph's wing-case.
19. Whip finish and coat it with black head-cement.

Fig 24 Making a weighted underbody

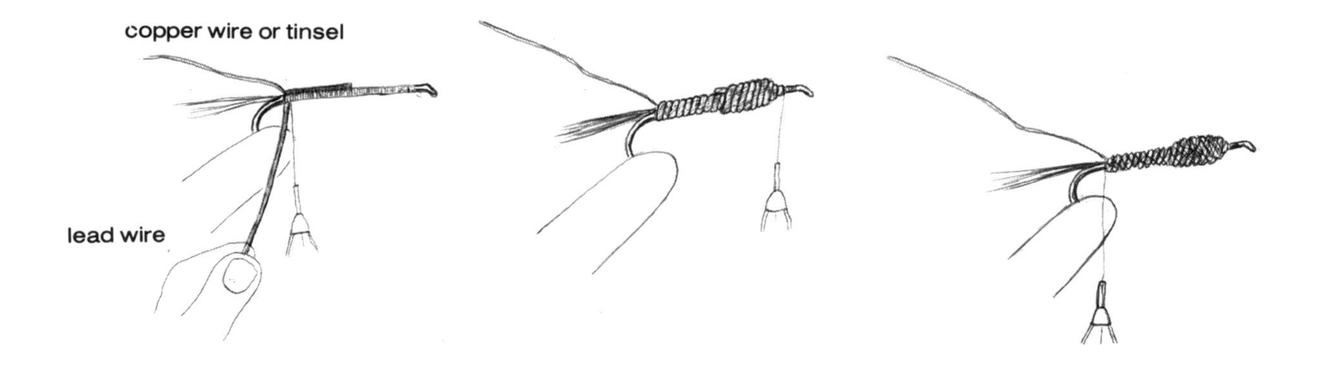

Fig 25 Making a dubbed fur body

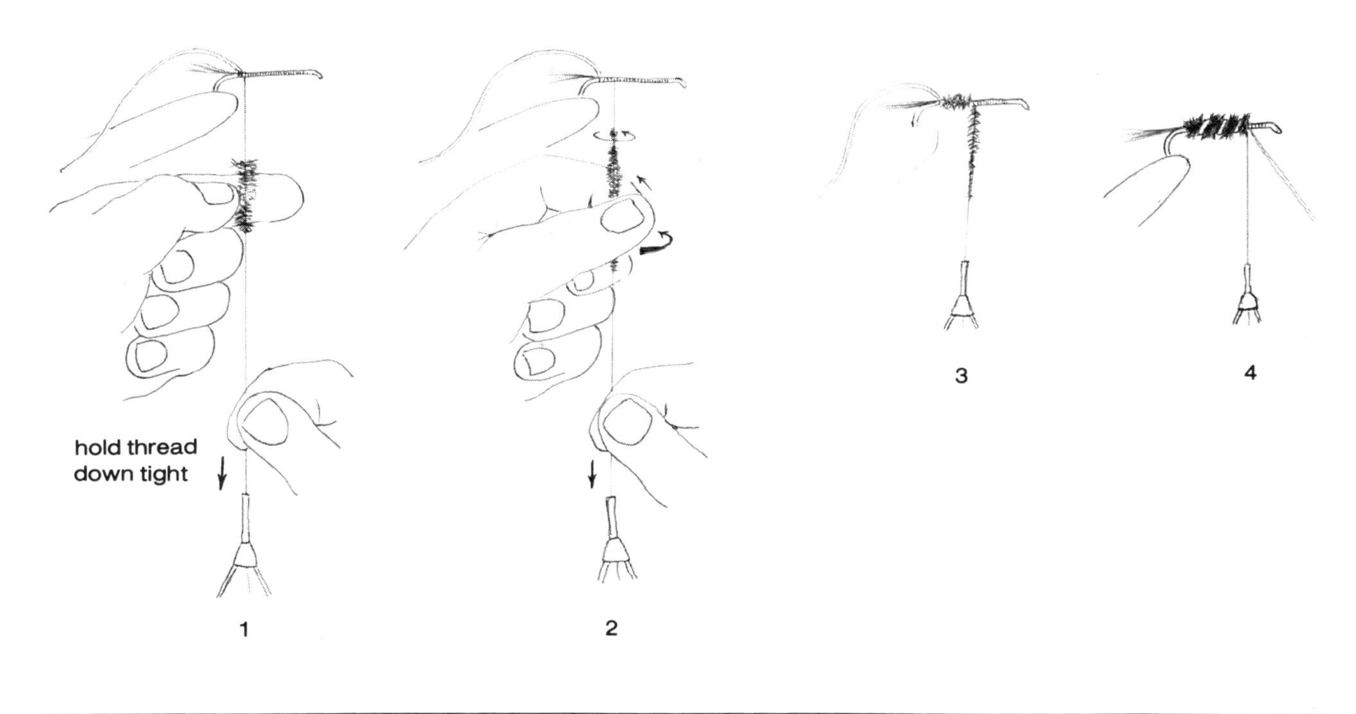

Now here are a few of my favourite nymph patterns. Paradoxically, the first one isn't a nymph at all, but a larva, the difference being that an insect which, on hatching, is an approximate replica of the eventual imago or adult is known as a "nymph", and one which emerges from the egg in a totally different shape to the parents is a "larva". For example, cockroaches or grasshoppers hatch more or less as miniature adults (nymphs), while butterflies start off as caterpillars and bluebottles as maggots (larvae).

However, since the caddis larva is fished exactly the same way as a nymph and is referred to as a nymph by most anglers anyway, I've included it here. I don't suppose it's any worse than calling a Grey Ghost an artificial *fly* when in reality it's actually an artificial *fish*, or referring to houseflies, spiders, ants, moths and beetles collectively as "bugs".

The hook I've recommended for this first pattern, Mustad 37160, is an odd-crank-shanked variety I haven't mentioned before. If you're on a really tight budget, you can get away with

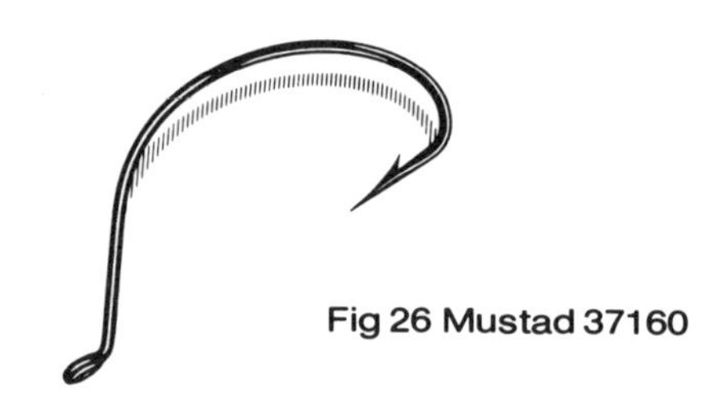

Fig 26 Mustad 37160

slightly bending the shank of a Mustad 9672 instead.

CADDIS LARVA (N)

Mustad 37160 hooks, sizes 12–16
Strip of cream or pale-green latex rubber
White floss
Lead wire
Yellow Monocord
Peacock herl
Clear body-cement

Bind the hook shank with thread and tie in white floss and latex rubber. Wind thread back up almost to the eye, tie in lead wire and wind thread back to where you began. Wind lead wire around the shank in closely lapping turns down to thread, trim and then wind thread back up over it to about 2 mm from the eye. Coat lead with cement and bind over with floss until hidden, then tie off floss and coat again with cement. Now stretch the latex and wind in overlapping turns over the floss until it is completely covered, then bind end securely down and trim. This binding *must* be secure, otherwise the latex will pull out. Tie in a strand of peacock herl and give it one or two turns round the remaining space to provide a little head. Complete with a whip finish. The result should be a good imitation of a semi-opaque little caddis larva who has lost his house and will hopefully be discovered tumbling helplessly downstream by a hungry trout. I have a friend who ties a variation he calls the Silkworm. Dubbing some fine, pale fur on to the body before winding on the latex, he ensures that some of the fibres are trapped by – and protrude between – each latex overlap, thus

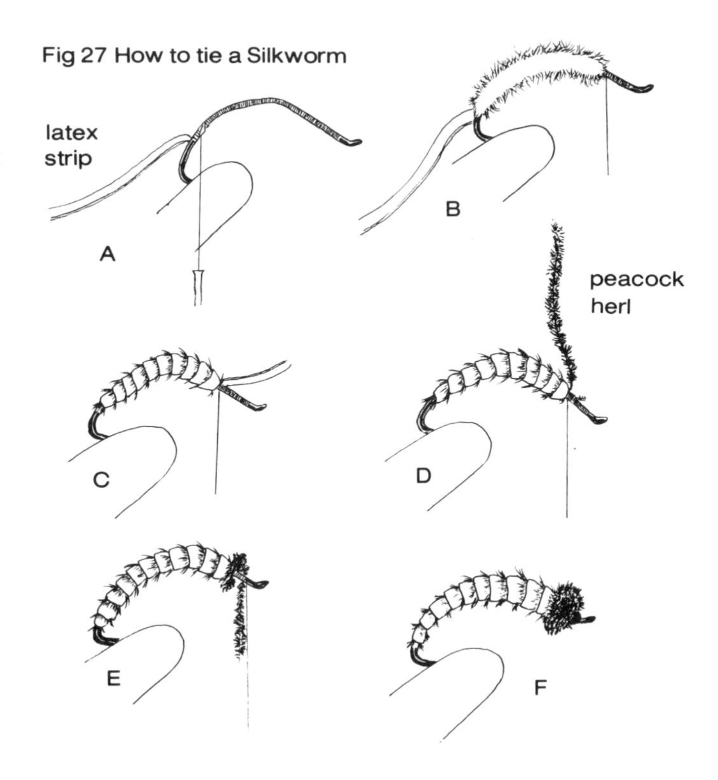

Fig 27 How to tie a Silkworm

giving the completed fly a sort of overall silky appearance. This version certainly works better for him than it does for me, but since I only discovered his secret a short time ago I haven't been able to give it a fair trial yet. Next season . . . .

SILKWORM (N) (A silky-bodied latex caddis larva)

A shows the hook shank bound with thread and latex strip tied in. If you require a weighted version add lead wire, cement it and cover with an overbinding of white or yellow floss as described in directions for tying the standard version. Using a white or creamy fur, form a good, shaggy dubbed body over the floss as shown in B.

Wind latex strip under tension up the body in overlapping turns, making sure plenty of fibres are caught between and protrude from each overlapping segment (C). Tie down about 2 mm from the eye, and tie in a strand of peacock herl (D). Fill up the empty 2 mm with a few turns of herl (E), tie in, trim surplus, whip-finish and cement. The finished larva (F) looks exceptionally good when wet, the fur fibres which shroud the body adding a dramatic translucent overall effect.

HALFBACK (N)

Mustad 9672 hooks, sizes 10–16
Green or bronze peacock herl
Fine copper wire
Mallard primaries or dark rubber strip
Small soft, webby ginger feather
Cock pheasant tail feather
Lead wire
Wonder Wax
Black Monocord

I first came across this pattern many years ago in the Kamloops region of British Columbia, where it

Caddis Larvae

Hare and Copper

Halfback

Amber Swannundaze

Hughie's Bug

Black Nymph

NYMPHS

Black Gnat

Greenwell's Glory

Mallard and Claret

Coch-y-bondhu

Butcher

Blue Dun

REGULAR WEE WET FLIES

was tied on extremely long-shanked hooks in sizes from 4 down to 8 and fished as a wet fly! I don't know what it was supposed to represent, but I caught a lot of fish with it in Lac Le Jeune, casting downwind from a drifting dinghy. Here in New Zealand it has reappeared in recent years in a much smaller version as a nymph and as such is fished upstream in rivers.

Bind the hook shank with thread and tie in lead if required. Tie in a few cock pheasant tail fibres to produce a tail about half the length of the body. Tie in one end of the copper wire and 2 or 3 strands of peacock herl. Wax about 9 cm (4 in) of tying thread and twist the herls around it to form a "rope" which is then wound halfway up the hook shank and secured with a couple of turns of thread. Tie in feather segment or rubber strip for wing-case and repeat the herl "rope-trick" to form rest of body. Spiral copper all the way up to give added protection to the fragile peacock herl. Now tie in a ginger hackle feather and give one or two turns, binding the thread to hold fibres sloping back at 45° and then bring the wing-case over the top, secure, whip-finish the head and cement.

HARE AND COPPER (N)

Mustad 9672 hooks, sizes 10–16
Hare's fur (the coarse dark outer hair is best)
Fine copper wire
Lead wire if required
Wonder Wax
Yellow Monocord

This is one of the simplest of all nymph patterns to tie and is universally effective. It's a particularly good one for beginners, since even the most clumsily tied one works well. In fact I sometimes think the most ragged and untidy specimens work best of all!

Bind the hook shank with thread and add lead wire if required. Tie in a short pinch of "hare's hair" for a tail, then tie in one end of the fine copper wire. (If a lightly weighted nymph is required, leave off the lead and use a heavier grade of copper wire in lieu of the fine.) Wax 9 cm (4 in) or so of the tying thread to dub on a really good shaggy hare's-fur body. Spiral the copper wire up over it as double security, finish at the head and apply head cement. That's it!

You can embellish and alter this pattern in many different ways. Some people tie in a longer tail using 4 or 5 cock pheasant tail feathers, add a wing-case or use a few turns of brown partridge to provide speckled "legs". The results may look better to the angler, but I doubt if the trout will notice any difference, the secret of its success appearing to lie in the coarse, hairy body.

HUGHIE'S BUG (N)

Mustad 9672 hooks, sizes 10–16
Any colour Monocord
Lead wire
Fine copper wire
Brown or black latex strip
Speckled brown partridge feather
Muddy brownish-grey darning wool
Cock pheasant tail fibres

Bind hook shank with thread and tie in a tail using 3 or 4 cock pheasant tail fibres so they extend perhaps 6 mm ($\frac{1}{4}$ in) or so from the rear. Tie in end of copper wire and end of wool. If required, tie in lead wire and wrap three quarters of the way up shank and two or three times back over itself, lash with thread and saturate with cement. When cement has gone tacky wind thread up to doubled lead, bind wool up (to make the body) and secure it about halfway up hook shank. Spiral the copper wire up over the top, secure and trim. Tie in end of latex wing-case, bring thread up to near the eye, then use remainder of wool to create the thorax. Secure with thread and trim. Tie in partridge feather (see fig. 28) and give it a few turns round the hook shank, then secure with thread and trim. (Be careful when using these delicate feathers because they are extremely fragile, and if you try to wind too tightly they will inevitably break.)

Fig 28 Tying in a partridge feather

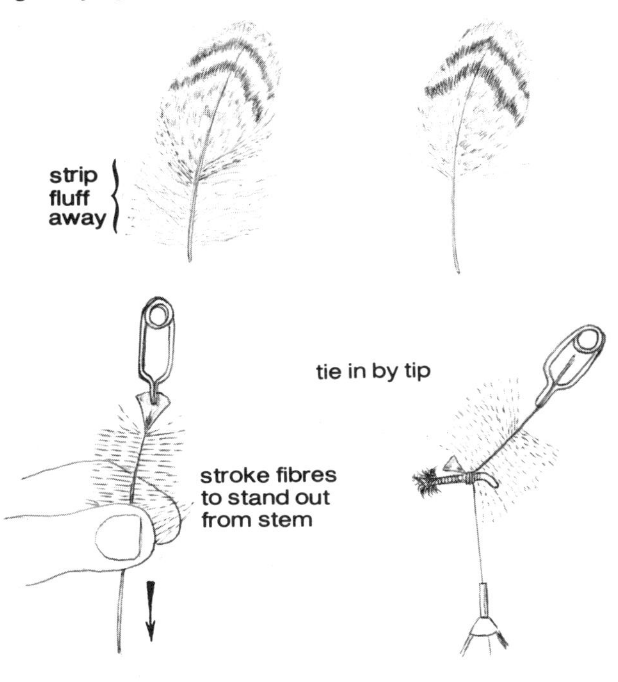

Wind thread back to hold the fibres sloping at 45°, Hackle-style. Bring latex over the top and secure end under whip finish and cement.

This is a cracker of a nymph which I used to fish exclusively. I used wool for the body because I had trouble making good dubbed-fur bodies, but the particular brand of wool (Spinnerin "Toros") I used eventually went off the market and partridge feathers became both difficult and expensive to obtain. Then I discovered "Wonder Wax" which made dubbed fur a piece of cake, so I changed over to tying and using Hare and Coppers which seemed to work just as well. However, having caught so many fish on the original pattern I still have a feeling of insecurity if I find myself on a strange river without a few of my old favourites in my fly box, so any time I come across some brown speckled partridge feathers, I hunt up a suitably drab piece of wool and tie up a dozen or so.

The name originated in Northern California where I used to tie flies for my local tackle shop, and this nymph of mine was a particularly popular one. For want of a better name I'd originally called it "March Brown", but it was so much more successful than the crude commercial ties under that name that customers started asking for "that bug of Hughie's". Years later I was amused to see a similar creation in rival sports stores under the names "Shoebug" and "Q-bug". Such are the origins of trout-fly names.

These few nymphs in assorted sizes and weights are about all I use nowadays, but if you like you can experiment with different-coloured dubbed-fur bodies, or combinations of floss bodies, fur or herl thoraxes and various feathers to produce an almost endless permutation of patterns. However, I feel that in the long run it is the way the nymph is presented to the fish that is the real clincher rather than the actual pattern – most of the time anyway.

In the years before the Wheao was ruthlessly and needlessly destroyed by the authorities in their insatiable search for unnecessary surplus hydro-power, I used to regularly fish its crystal pools and runs with two friends, Ken and Mark. We'd often fish in turns with a couple of us spotting from the high bank and calling out to the third where to place his nymph, because from the relatively high vantage point big trout could often be observed which were invisible to the angler in the water. When a fish was taken, one of the spotters would trade positions with the angler, and so we'd fish as a team. In those days I almost always used a Hughie's Bug, while Ken favoured a Hare's Ear and Mark stuck to a Halfback, but despite the fact that we were all using different nymphs, we all seemed to end up catching and releasing about the same number of trout. Remember, everything everybody did always had two witnesses, so there were no tall stories to take into consideration!

You learn as much from "spotting" as you do from actually fishing, and from my experience at both I am firmly convinced that where nymphs are concerned presentation is considerably more important than pattern.

Wet Flies

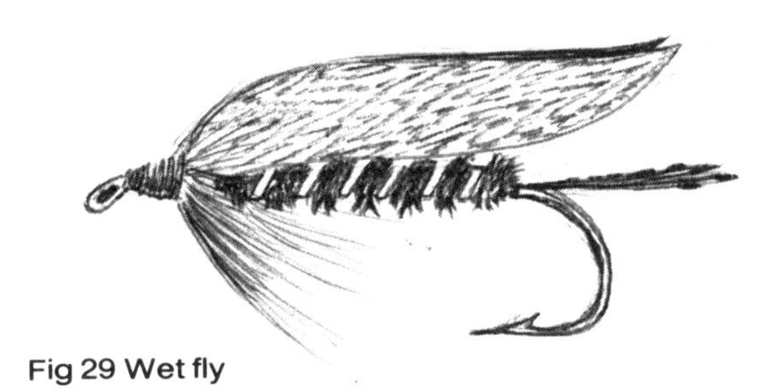

Fig 29 Wet fly

"Only God can make a tree" goes the verse of the old song, but when you look through a magnifying glass at the intricate structure of an aquatic insect, you are tempted to replace the word "tree" with "fly" and marvel at the audacity of anyone attempting to create an artificial replica.

Yet, crude as our attempts may be, flies that regularly fool trout *can* be tied. The answer, of course, lies in not trying to make an exact imitation but rather in producing an illusion of what the trout *expects* to see. Thus, if friend trout is feeding on small black nymphs struggling to emerge from their nymphal shucks as they are being swept down over the bubbling shallows, a small black wet fly of approximately the same size is very likely to be mistaken for the real thing in the brief period it is in view, because that's what he's expecting.

For example, if I take a box of eggs and throw nine of them at a wall they will, of course, smash and the yolks will run down the brickwork making a mess. If I then toss you the tenth one, which is a crude china dummy, you will catch it very gingerly, because you *expect* it to be real and in the short time available for inspection you have not spotted it as an imitation. Yet if I show you the box of eggs and ask you to pick the dummy, you can do it right away.

So it is with artificial flies, and with small wet flies perhaps more than any other type you should aim at keeping them as sparsely dressed as possible to help maintain the illusion of reality. A lightly dubbed fur body and a few wispy hackles will provide a far better suggestion of the real thing than the bushy, overdressed patterns so many commercial tyers produce. Of course, not all wet flies are made to represent living insects. Some are purely "attractor" patterns and don't look like anything on earth. Perhaps they are taken out of curiosity or even anger, nobody really knows for sure, but the fact remains that they will sometimes work when all else fails. And, if you like to fish with two flies, it can be a good idea to have an attractor pattern on the dropper.

I can only remember ever once identifying a trout's stomach contents with an attractor fly, and that was in Scotland's Loch Ness many years ago. I'd gone out with a local policeman in his boat very early in the morning, and though the trout were rising everywhere all around us, none of the regular tried and true flies he recommended drew the least bit of interest. In despair I tied on a Bloody Butcher, a great favourite in Ireland, and this did the trick, accounting for some 28 fish between us before the rise finished. When I was cleaning the six best ones we'd kept, I found all without exception were stuffed literally to the gills with small red "bloodworms" which are the larvae of a variety of European midges (called "Harlequin flies") and which swim very actively through the water by rapidly coiling and uncoiling their red worm-like bodies. I can only presume that the blood-red hackle of our Bloody Butchers bore enough resemblance to the blood-red colour of the larvae to fool the trout, but what they made of the royal blue wing and the silver tinsel body I really don't know!

Wet flies are tied both with and without wings. We'll begin by tying a simple "spider" pattern, as the unwinged variety is called.

HOW TO TIE A SIMPLE WET FLY

For this one you'll need:
 Mustad 9672 size 12 hook
 Cock pheasant tail fibres
 Black floss
 Medium oval tinsel (gold or silver)
 A small, webby black feather
 Black Monocord

1. Secure hook in vice. Lay thread along shank from A to B and wind back over itself to A. Let bobbin holder dangle between stages.
2. Take 3 or 4 fibres from cock pheasant tail. Secure thick ends at A with 3 or 4 turns of thread. Trim surplus with scissors.
3. Secure end of piece of floss silk with 2–3 turns of thread at A and trim surplus with scissors.
4. Repeat process with piece of tinsel.
5. Wind thread up shank to B.
6. Wind floss silk up shank in close even turns. Secure at B with 2–3 turns of thread. Trim surplus with scissors.
7. Wind tinsel over floss silk in wide spiral (3 or 4 turns) securing at B with 2–3 turns of thread. Trim surplus with scissors.
8. Strip fluff from stem of hackle feather and secure stem at B with 2–3 turns of thread.
9. Grip tip of feather with hackle pliers and wind round and round at B. Tie tip down with 2–3 turns of thread. Trim surplus with scissors.
10. Now hold hackle fibres back parallel to hook shank and wind thread back over them until they lie at 45° angle. Whip-finish head. A drop of head-cement will help prevent unravelling.

You can use this technique with different materials and colours to create a wide variety of patterns. Try slim dubbed-fur or peacock herl

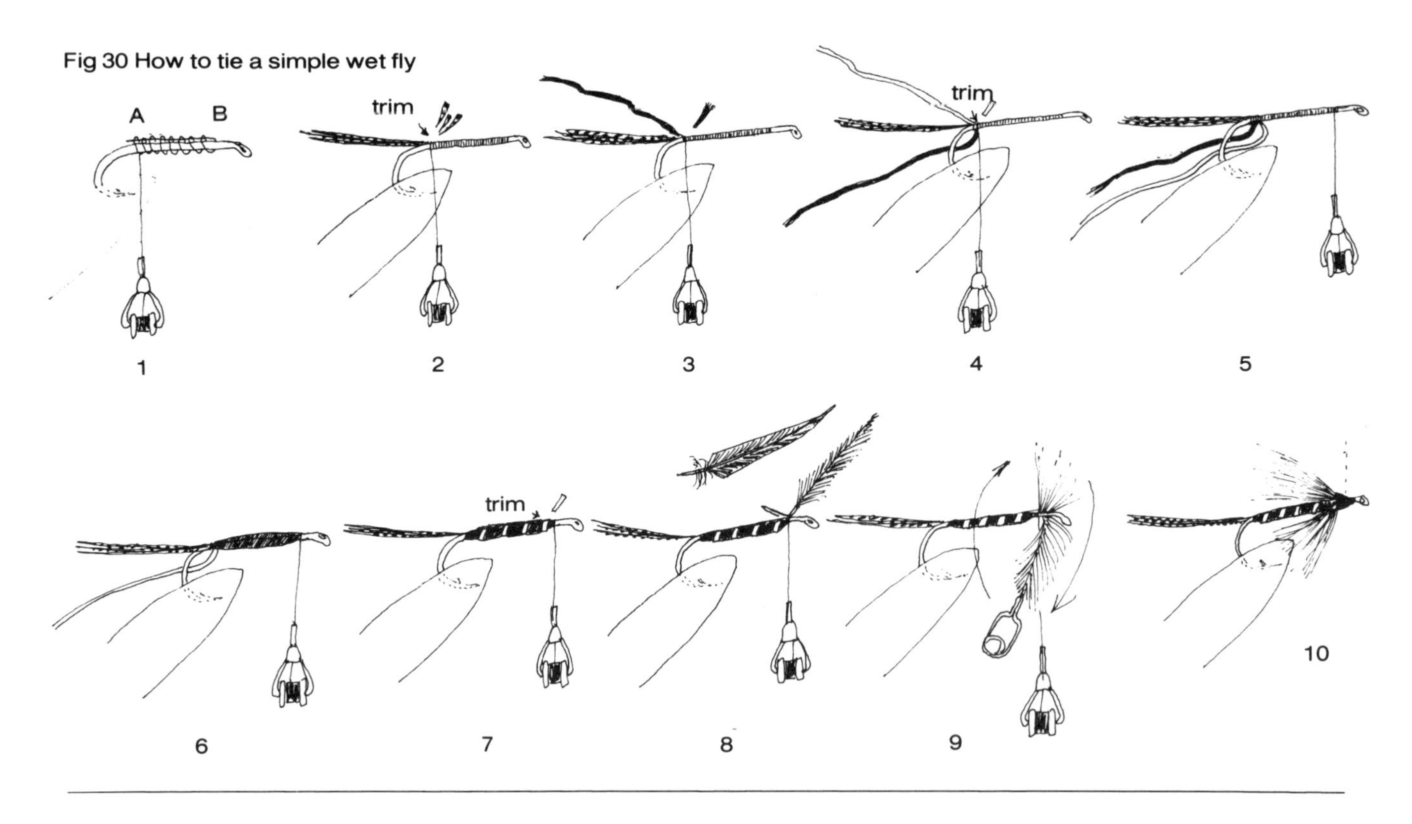

Fig 30 How to tie a simple wet fly

bodies and ginger or furnace hackles, or you might like to use a brown speckled partridge feather instead (see fig. 28).

When you can confidently produce simple, effective spiders, move on to the next chapter, and we'll take a look at how to add wings if and when required.

WINGED WET FLIES

There are really two types of wings used on little wet flies, namely primary feather strips and feather-fibre bunches. The latter is nothing more than a small bunch of appropriate fibres tied in at the head of the fly before whip-finishing the completed fly, but the former is a little more difficult to master. Here's how I go about it.

When you reach stage 7 (see fig. 30) leave the bobbin holder dangling while you cut a small slip from a primary wing feather as you did for the

Fig 31 Winging a wet fly

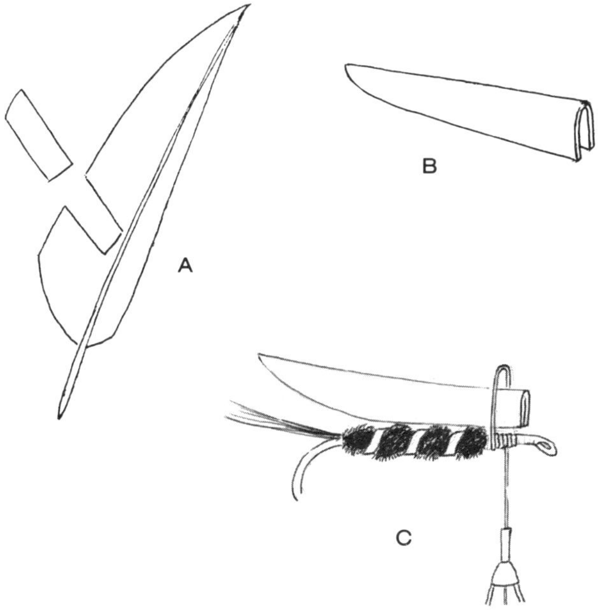

A

B

C

Continued over . . .

Fig 31 continued

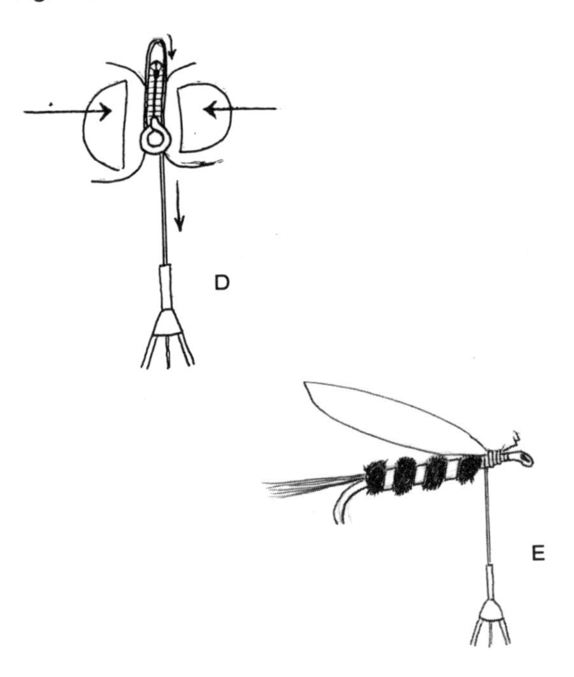

nymph's wing-case (fig. 23). The exact size depends on the size of the hook used, but 6 mm ($\frac{1}{4}$ in) or so should be about right. Fold this over (B), hold on top of the hook shank, folded side upwards, and the cut end towards the eye, so as to make the wing about the same length as the body (C). Squeeze the two portions of feather tightly together and bring the thread back between your finger and thumb before coming down the other side of the hook shank (D), just as you learned to do when putting the tail on a Hackle-style lure earlier on (fig. 6).

Repeat this several times and the loops you formed between your finger and thumb should have pulled the end of the feather-slip tightly down to secure it firmly to the hook shank, so the wing slopes back in a flat vertically-sided way rather like a resting butterfly's wings do (E).

Now carry on at stage 8 and complete your fly.

The following is a list of some of the more popular wet flies. I use Mustad 9672 hooks from size 10 to 16 for all of them.

BUTCHER (W)

Tail: bunch of dyed-red hackle fibres
Body: flat silver Mylar tinsel
Wing: slip of the iridescent blue feather from a mallard's wing
Hackle: soft black

This is an old attractor pattern which still works well. Its cousin the Bloody Butcher, which features dyed red hackle instead of black, is very popular in Ireland for both resident and sea-run brownies.

I have a very soft spot for the Bloody Butcher since the very first time I caught a trout on the fly it was with this pattern.

BLUE DUN (W)

Tail: bunch of fibres from same feather as hackle
Body: dubbed fur (mole or muskrat are good choices)
Wing: slip of primary wing feather from starling or blackbird
Hackle: smoky blue-grey

Although I'm not persuaded that as a general rule there is much of a need for a terribly great range of wet flies, the Blue Dun is one which, when it's "on", will be the *only* fly to use. My friend Nigel regularly catches fish with a Blue Dun wet fly when fish are feeding on emerging caddis in the famous Kaituna Trout Pool near Rotorua. Why this should work I haven't the foggiest idea since the Blue Dun bears no resemblance colour-wise to the greenish-bodied naturals. But work it does (for him anyway!) so who am I to argue? Try it for yourself.

BLACK GNAT (W)

Tail: a few fibres of black feather
Body: black ostrich herl or dubbed black fur
Wing: slip of starling or blackbird primary wing feather
Hackle: soft black

I am not sure what this is supposed to represent, but it has taken plenty of fish for me over the years. The dark silhouette makes it a good choice for discoloured water conditions.

BLOODY BUTCHER (W)

(See BUTCHER)

GREENWELL'S GLORY (W)

Tail: (optional) 3 or 4 golden pheasant tippets
Body: primrose floss ribbed with fine gold wire or tinsel
Wing: slip of primary wing feather from mallard, blackbird or starling
Hackle: furnace hackle

This is an exceptionally good all-round pattern and one which I am never without, having taken more fish on it than almost any other, except perhaps the March Brown.

The best day's fishing I have ever had, or indeed am likely ever to have again, was with a Greenwell's Glory. I'll tell you about it, and, although you probably won't believe me, I can assure you it is true.

One morning in 1969 I went fishing with my friend Ed Volpe (from the "Rotodyeran" episode referred to earlier in this book) in a Northern California limestone stream called Hat Creek. It was a grey, overcast, blustery day, and the fishing was poor, to say the least. In fact, it was so poor that by lunchtime neither of us had touched a fish. Ed used the dry fly, but I was fishing a couple of wets when I eventually hooked a small fish on a March Brown. I saw Ed change his fly but didn't take much notice until he too hooked a fish, then another and another. Since I wasn't having any more action I asked him what he was using, and he said that when I got the first fish on a wet fly, he decided to try wets himself and had tied on a little Greenwell's Glory I'd given him once for a pattern. Quickly I dug into my fly box and located another one just like it, and, knotting it on to my leader, spat on it for luck before casting it just upstream of a trout which had conveniently started to rise nearby. There was a glint of gold, a splashy swirl and with a tug I was fast to the first good fish of the day. By the time I had played it out, unhooked and released it a good rise was underway, and I wasted no time in covering the nearest one. This fish also took without hesitation, as did the next, and the next. In fact, for the rest of the afternoon *every* rising fish that we presented those little Greenwells to seized them as though they had been waiting for one all their lives. I've never seen anything like it, honestly. Every trout came to the fly as surely as a pin comes to a magnet. We fished our way back to the car where Ed quit fishing for the day — he was just plain "fished out", he told me later. But I couldn't stop, it was all too impossibly glorious, and I fished on into the summer dusk, right up to the last minute of the regulation "one hour after sunset" that marked the legal end of the Northern California fishing day, and I was in a daze of delight when I rejoined Ed back at the car.

Driving home, we tried to remember the number of trout we'd caught, and he reckoned he'd had around 40. I lost count somewhere about 50, and to this day I really don't know how many it was, but we both agreed it must have been around 80-odd.

Of course, I've never had anything like that happen since, but on many occasions a small wet Greenwell's Glory has been a real winner for me when the madly rising trout seemed disinterested in all the dry flies I floated over them. Try one next time there's a good rise to caddis going on in the riffles, and you can't seem to connect. I don't know why, but for some reason this is one pattern that frequently works particularly well in this situation.

COCH-Y-BONDHU (W)

Body: peacock herl
Hackle: dark furnace

The original pattern featured "coch-y-bondhu" hackle (black-tipped furnace) which you can't get nowadays and a couple of turns of fine gold tinsel on the shank before the body commences. I leave the tinsel off altogether and use ordinary dark furnace for the hackle without any appreciable difference to the fly's fish-catching ability.

A good choice for murky water when the river is clearing after a flood.

MARCH BROWN (W)

Tail: cock pheasant tail feather fibres
Body: dubbed hare's fur, sometimes ribbed with fine oval gold tinsel
Wing: slip of mottled brown feather from a hen pheasant wing
Hackle: speckled brown partridge

The drab hues of the March Brown give a good general impression of a great many forms of aquatic life and make it an excellent choice where you're not sure what the trout may be feeding on.

For this reason I often tie it without wings when it is probably taken as an emerging nymph.

MALLARD FLIES (W)

The mallard flies are basically attractor flies, and though they are as old as the hills they will still take their share of trout today, although you don't see them offered for sale as you once used to.

Once you have finished the body, tie in a bunch of bronze mallard feather fibres as a wing and then add the hackle.

MALLARD AND ORANGE (W)

Tail: golden pheasant tippets
Body: dubbed orange seal's fur with oval gold tinsel rib
Hackle: soft pale ginger

I used the Mallard and Orange with great success on Northern California's Klamath River for steelhead and have taken many trout in New Zealand on it, too.

MALLARD AND RED (W)

As above but with red seal's fur.

MALLARD AND CLARET (W)

As above but with claret seal's fur and either claret or black hackle.

I have also found this tied with pale ginger hackle to be a good killing fly in some Hawkes Bay rivers and in weedy lakes like Otamangakau near Turangi or Aniwhenua near Murupara.

TEAL FLIES (W)

Like mallard flies these are all very old patterns which fall into the "attractor" category, and I've caught fish on all of them at one time or another.

Having finished the body, tie in a bunch of the speckled black and white barred fibres from a teal's flank feather as a wing, then complete the fly by adding the hackle.

If you can't get teal feathers there are similar ones on a paradise duck's flank.

TEAL AND ORANGE (W)

Tail: golden pheasant tippets
Body: dubbed orange seal's fur with oval gold tinsel rib
Hackle: pale soft ginger

TEAL AND RED (W)

As above but with red seal's fur and oval silver tinsel.

TEAL AND SILVER (W)

Tail: golden pheasant tippets
Body: flat silver Mylar tinsel
Hackle: sapphire blue

DRY FLIES

Fig 32 Winged dry fly

I don't know why, but for some reason the concept of tying a dry fly seems to strike terror into the hearts of more beginners than does any other type of fly. Perhaps it's because for so long dry-fly anglers have tended to be a haughty bunch who kept aloof from lesser mortals, shopped only at Hardy's and called flies by their Latin names, that they've created an air of mystique and superiority around their craft.

I have no such illusions about it, and neither should you. Let's face it, of all the forms of fly-fishing, the dry fly is the easiest to learn. You're usually fishing upstream, so you can get closer to the fish and don't have to cast far. Both the line and the fly are floating, you can see the trout actually take your fly, and you don't have to react particularly quickly. What could be easier?

Likewise, tying a simple dry fly is a piece of cake compared to, say, a Killer-type lure. A simple tail, a body, a few turns of hackle and presto! One perfectly satisfactory dry fly. "Ah but . . ." I can hear you say, "you mentioned capes of feathers that cost $100 – and I'll need several colours, too. I can't afford that sort of outlay, especially if I'm going to make a lot of mistakes!" True. I've been tying flies for over 30 years, and I've only ever owned one $100 cape – and that was given to me.

Red-tipped Governor

Blue Dun

Peveril of the Peak

Adams

Royal Wulff

Twilight Beauty

Probably the most effective of all the "wee wets" are the simple, easy-to-tie ones, which undoubtedly give a fair impression of a dun struggling to escape from its nymphal shuck. For this reason they are best fished just under the surface, across and downstream, using a floating or a slow sink-tip line. You'll find a description of how to tie one on page 113, but the five shown here illustrate how you can use the same technique to create many different variations, simply by using different materials.

What I said earlier was that you should get the best you can afford, and you can get a perfectly satisfactory quality for 10 per cent of the price of a top quality one. I want to stress once again, however, that the better the quality of the feathers, the better the finished product will float. I can assure you that tying a dry fly with cheap webby hackles and then drenching it in fly-floatant just doesn't work. All that so-called "fly-floatant" can do is make the materials more water-repellent, but it can't, and it won't, provide the stiff, springy hackle fibres necessary to support the fly on the surface. Only quality feathers can do this.

Just as an exercise, however, suppose you *did* splash out and buy a $100 "Metz" or "Hoffman" cape. You'd be able to tie at least 300 superb dry flies from it, even allowing for mistakes – and you'd have plenty of big feathers left over for lake lures at that. That works out at 33 cents a fly, and if you add, say, 5 cents for a hook and other materials, that's 38 cents and I'll bet you're paying *double* that for your commercially tied dry flies right now, and at that price I can guarantee they aren't tied with top-grade hackle! So if you take a good-quality hook and a good-quality hackle you can tie a dry fly with a dubbed belly-button lint body if you like – and catch fish on it, too. It's the hackles that count.

HOW TO TIE A SIMPLE DRY FLY

Let's tie a simple dry fly right now, so you can see just how easy it really is.

You'll need:
A Mustad 9672 size 14 hook
Black Monocord
Peacock herl
Fine oval tinsel
"Wonder Wax"
A good-quality dry-fly cape (I don't think it matters what colour, but if you like we'll use furnace)

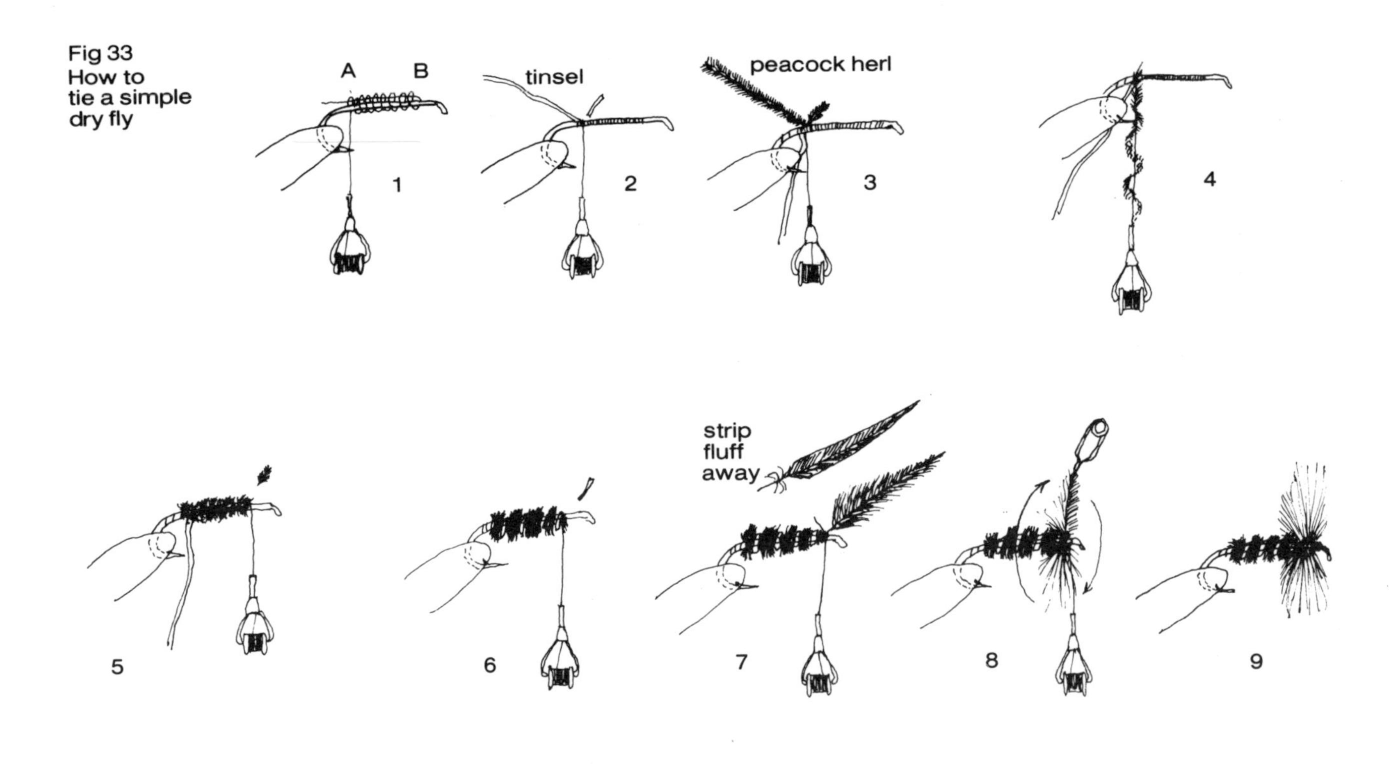

Fig 33
How to tie a simple dry fly

1. Secure hook in vice and bind shank from B to A.
2. Tie in tinsel.
3. Tie in peacock herl.
4. Twist herl round waxed thread.
5. With the end of the herl held tightly to the thread to prevent it unwinding, wind the herl rope up the shank in close turns to form a plump body, but stop before you reach B to leave plenty of room for the hackles. If you haven't used up all the herl at this stage, carefully wind the surplus from the thread back down to the hook shank. Secure end of body windings with several turns of thread and clip off surplus herl.
6. Spiral tinsel up body, secure and trim surplus.
7. Wind thread on up shank to B using close, even turns. Pluck a feather from your dry fly cape. Choose one on which most of the hackle fibres are approximately the same length as the body you've made. Strip all the fluffy, webby fibres from the bottom of the feather and then, holding the feather by its tip, stroke the remaining fibres downwards between the finger and thumb of your other hand. This will cause them to stand out at 90° from the stem (fig. 34). Hold the stem across the top of the

Fig 34

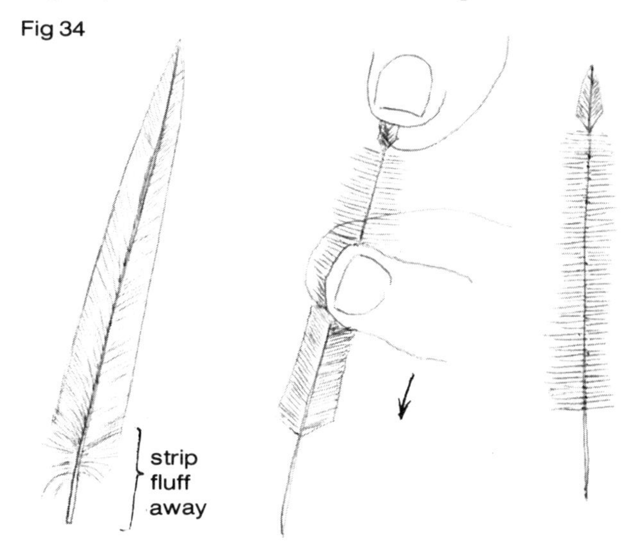

shank at B at right angles, with the tip pointing away from you and the shiny side of the hackles facing the front and secure with several turns of thread (fig. 35 steps 1A and 1B). Bend the stem back along the top of the shank (fig. 35 step 2) and bind it down, using very even, close turns of thread, until you reach the body (fig. 35 step 3).

8. Now leaving the bobbin holder dangling, grip the tip of the feather with your hackle pliers and wind it back to the body, using equally

Fig 35 Attaching the hackle to a dry fly

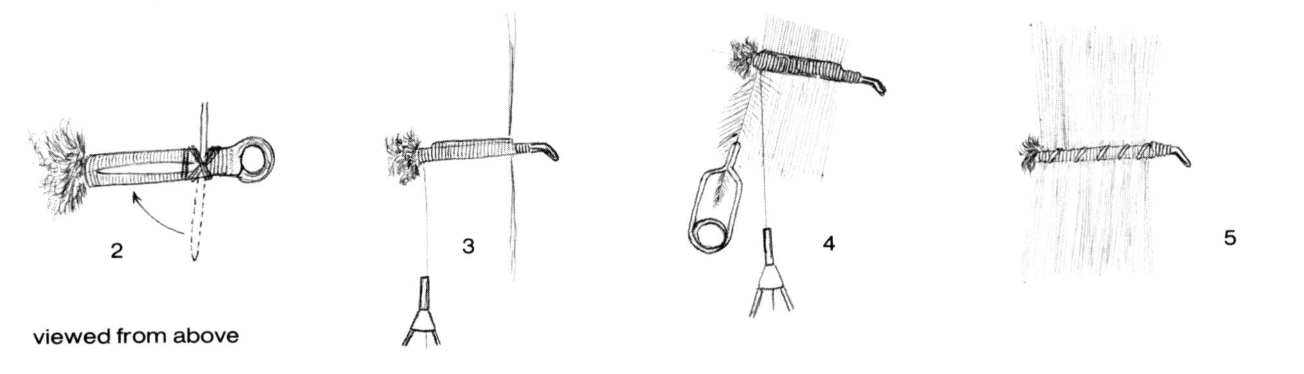

close, even turns, and tie in the end when you reach the body (fig. 35 step 4). If you've done this properly the hackle fibres will all be standing out at 90° from the hook shank.

9. After trimming away any surplus stem and tip, wind thread *carefully* through the forest of fibres back to B (fig. 35 step 5), whip finish and cement. If you've trapped any fibres in the process, they can be picked out with your dubbing needle.

This is a very simple pattern which will take fish regularly and is particularly effective in summer when the green beetle is up, but you can use the same technique with different ingredients to produce a whole myriad of patterns. Try adding a tail, using a bunch of hackle fibres or several cock pheasant tail fibres, before you start the body, which you can make with floss or dubbed fur if you like. There is no law that says you have to restrict your fly to only one hackle either, in fact I sometimes use up to four if I want to produce a particularly buoyant, bushy specimen, but, if you are going to do this, be sure to make the body just a little shorter than usual so as to leave enough room for the extra hackles.

Be inventive and experiment! Remember even the neatest fly you can tie is, at best, only a suggestion of the real thing and, as a general rule, the trout couldn't care less whether your imitation has three or four tail fibres or in fact whether or not it has a tail at all.

This also applies to wings. There is no doubt that winged artificials look more attractive and realistic to the angler, but I am of the firm opinion that they make little or no difference at all to the trout, despite what the experts say. Presentation, size and colour are the real keys to success with the dry fly and, to be honest, I rarely tie winged specimens at all nowadays.

However, I'll show you how to make them anyway, if for no other reason than that, by using highly visible materials, they will make your fly easier to spot in rough water or in poor light.

TYING A WINGED DRY FLY

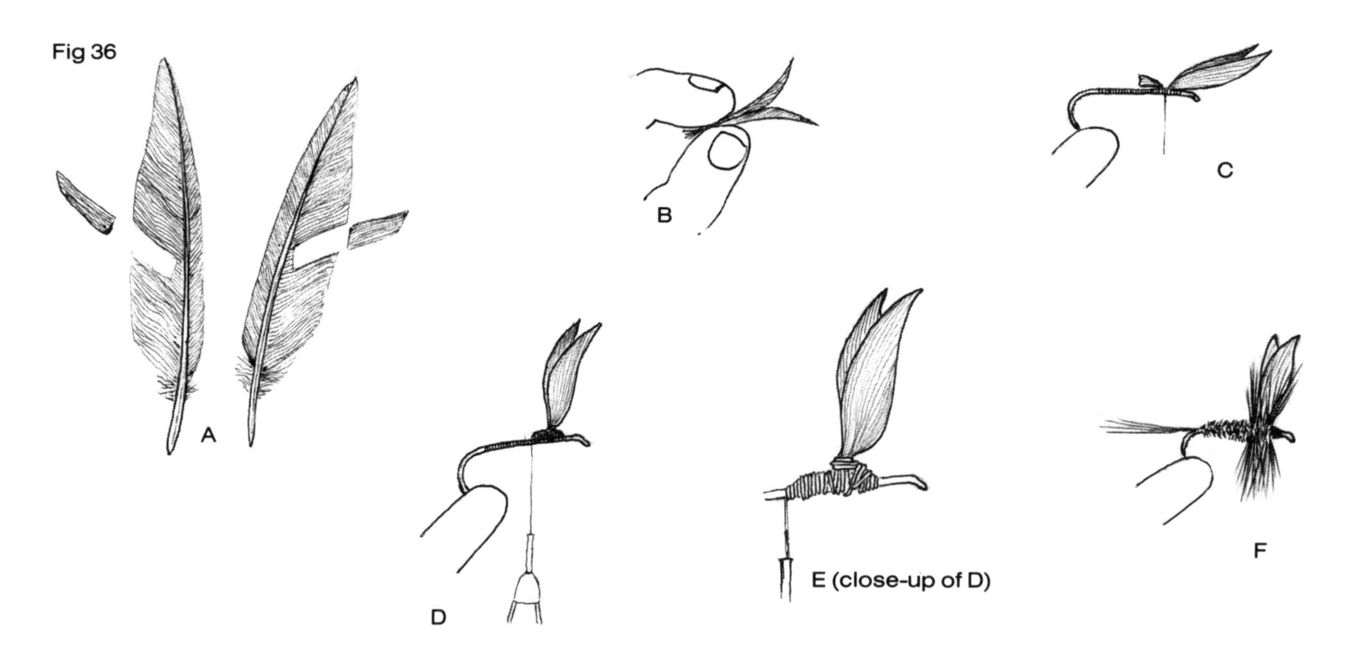

Bind shank with thread as usual, but bring thread back up about $\frac{2}{3}$ way of the shank.

Cut a sliver of feather about 3 mm ($\frac{1}{8}$ in) wide from both a right and a left wing feather (fig. 36 step A).

When you hold these together back to back with your left finger and thumb, they will curl away from each other as shown in fig. 36 step B.

Hold them horizontally on edge on top of the hook shank with tips forward over the eye and secure (as you learned to do with tails earlier on pages 26–7). The wings should now look like those shown in fig. 36 step C.

Grip wings with left finger and thumb and hold them vertically to hook shank while you build up a "shoulder" of thread in front to hold them there. A few turns around the bases at this stage may help as well (fig. 36 step D). Some tyers like to put a drop of clear cement right down between the bases, too, for added strength.

Fig. 36 step E shows a close-up of fig. 36 step D.

Now go on down to end of shank and tie in a tail, then form a body and bring it up to just short of wings.

Hackle can now be added as illustrated on pages 125–6 using a couple of turns ahead of the wings and the balance behind them, or you can use two feathers, completing one and then bringing the second over the same path so the hackles intermingle. Obviously you won't be able to bind the stems on top of the hook shank as you learned earlier due to the presence of the wings, so tie them along the sides or on the underside instead (see fig. 37).

Fig 37

If the pattern you're attempting calls for wings of hair or feather fibres, simply tie in a bunch of the material and bring up to vertical as before, then divide and separate by criss-crossing with thread in a figure-of-eight fashion until the desired angle is achieved (see fig. 38).

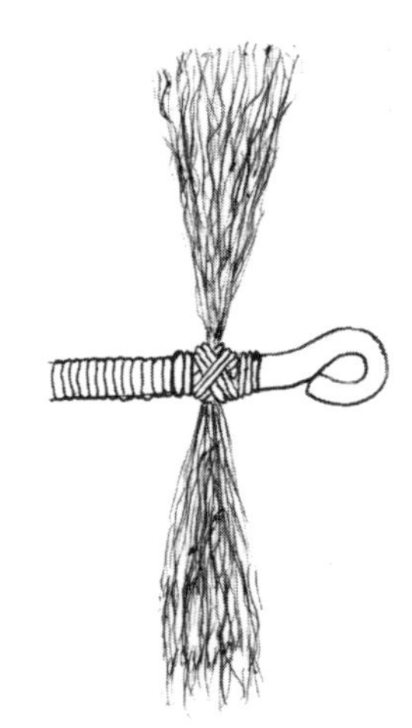

Fig 38

Now here are a few recipes for some of our most popular dry flies. The first one is an Adams, an old and very effective American pattern which has only recently been "discovered" by New Zealand anglers and is becoming increasingly popular. Since the tying technique differs slightly from what you've just learned, I've put it in at the beginning – which is just as well because alphabetically that's where it belongs anyway.

ADAMS (D)

Wings: tips of grizzle feathers as used for hackle
Body: dubbed mole, muskrat or other dark grey-blue fur
Hackle: 1 grizzle and 1 natural brown or ginger feather
Tail: mixed bunch of grizzle and brown fibres from same type of feathers as hackles

1. Bind hook shank with thread and tie in a bunch of mixed brown and grizzle hackle fibres for the tail, then wax the thread and dub on a fur body. Now tie in two matching grizzle

hackle tips for wings, shiny sides together, dull sides out and pointing forward as shown.

2. Pull wings back and hold them erect by several turns of thread against the butts, then wind thread criss-cross between them to separate and divide the wings.

3A. Shows view from above.

3B. Shows view from front.

4. Tie in one brown and one grizzle hackle, both pointing forward, then wind thread in as close even wraps as you can, back to the body.
5. Wind one hackle back to body, tie in and trim surplus tip.

Fig 39 How to tie an Adams dry fly

1

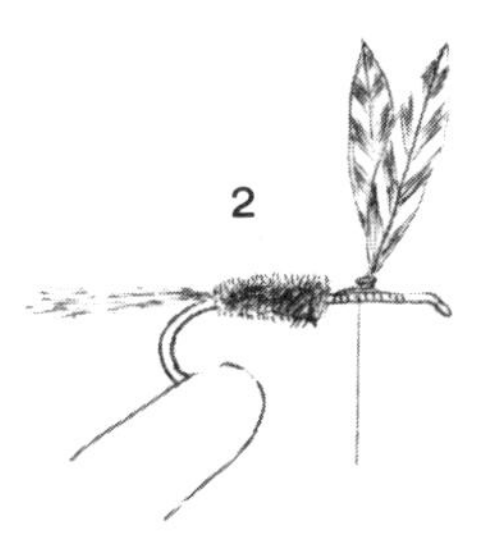

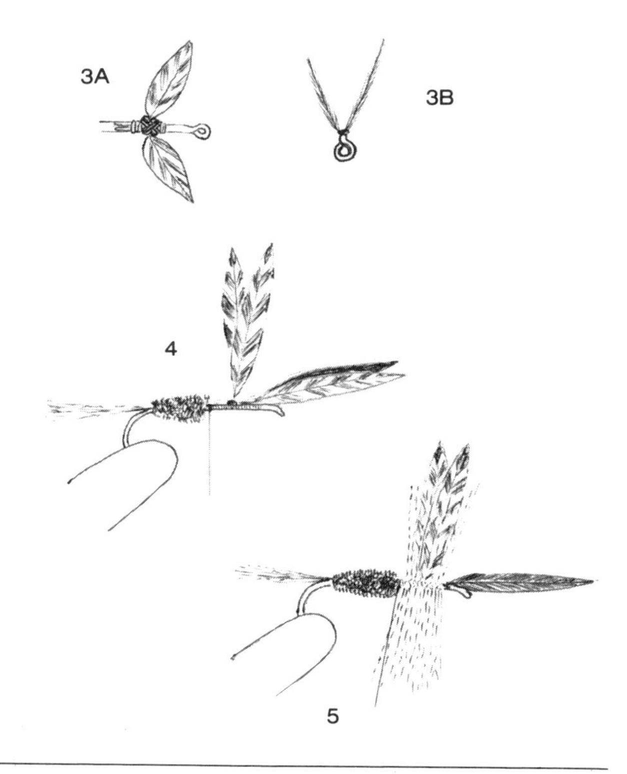

6. Wind remaining hackle carefully back through the first one to body, tie in and trim surplus tip. Now bring thread spiralling back through the hackle fibres to head, whip-finish and cement.

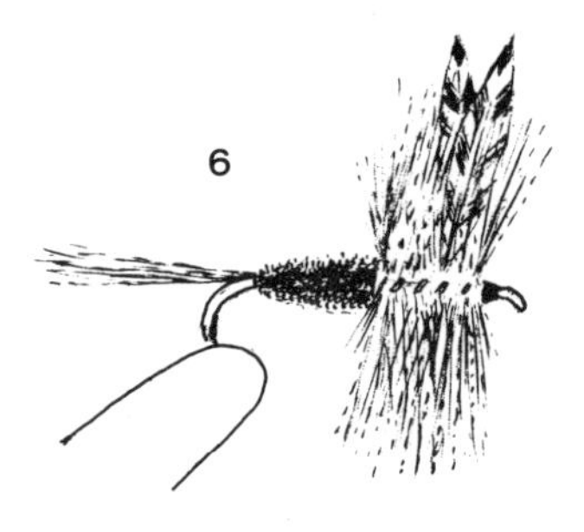

This is an extremely versatile and consistently effective American pattern which is rapidly gaining popularity in New Zealand. It makes a fair representation of a myriad of different mayflies and is an excellent choice when you can't identify what the trout are taking or if there doesn't appear to be any fly on the water. Indeed, it will often bring up trout when there is no rise at all! Like most of my dry flies, I leave off the wings altogether nowadays; although the results aren't as aesthetically pleasing, they work just as well.

BLACK GNAT (D)

Wings: slips from mallard, starling or blackbird primary wing feathers
Body: black dubbed fur
Hackle: black
Tail: bunch of black fibres from same type of feather as hackle

A good "general" imitation covering a whole range of aquatic insects and particularly useful in murky conditions. Just *how* effective was illustrated one sultry summer evening on the Manawatu near Palmerston North. The day's business finished, I was preparing my tackle in my motel room prior to taking a walk down the river for the evening rise when a colleague, who'd just checked in, spotted me at work through my open door. On learning I was going dry-fly fishing, Jay asked if he could come along to see how it was done as he'd never seen a fish taken in this manner, and I readily agreed. En route I remembered an earlier occasion when we'd met at Tokaanu where, on the first cast of his first attempt at fly fishing, he'd hooked and landed a magnificent 5 lb (2.27 kg) rainbow hen, and I wondered if he'd be as lucky on tonight's expedition.

It had rained a bit during the day, and I expected to find the river had risen a little, but I wasn't prepared for the chocolate-brown flood that greeted us on our arrival there. Hopeless as the conditions were, Jay insisted I show him how I'd have fished the dry fly anyway, so I had a few casts in a nearby riffle, demonstrating how to place the fly lightly upstream and retrieve line in pace with the floating fly's progress back toward the angler, explaining that under more favourable circumstances a trout could be expected to rise and take the fly, and following a second's pause to allow the fish to turn down with the prize, the line would be tightened by lifting the rod-tip and the trout subsequently hooked.

After watching for a few minutes he decided to have a practice at the technique himself and so put his rod, reel and line together. Like most beginners he'd had some difficulty "finding the fly" once it was cast on the water, so I handed him a big, bushy, highly visible Black Gnat. Of course, you can guess what happened. He cast lightly upstream, the fly cocked and rode jauntily for only a couple of feet when a nose appeared out of the thick cocoa-like murk and seized it. Jay counted, "One-two" out loud, struck gently and was into his first dry-fly-caught trout!

I'd like to say that after that we went on to have a great evening's fishing; as it happened we didn't, but it does show how the dark silhouette of the Black Gnat can be spotted by trout (and anglers!) even in the most adverse conditions.

BLUE DUN (D)

Wings: slips from primary wing feather of mallard, blackbird or starling
Body: dubbed greyish-blue fur but occasionally ribbed with a securing spiral of fine gold tinsel
Hackle: blue dun if you can get it or a dyed dark grey if you can't
Tail: bunch of fibres from same feathers as used for hackle

If you look at the majority of dry flies you'll find most of them are tied with either black, ginger, cream or brown hackle. Usually one of these colours in large, medium or small size will effect a reasonable facsimile of the natural mayfly on the water, but every now and then the rising trout will ignore all your tried and true favourites. When this happens to me I turn to the Blue Dun, and more often than not it does the trick when all the others have failed. Not a very scientific approach, perhaps, but who cares why it works so long as it does?

I have no doubt this statement will cause much gnashing of teeth among many of my angling friends, particularly those in South Island, for whom the Blue Dun is the *sine qua non* of dry flies, but I can only quote from my own personal experience.

COCH-Y-BONDHU (D)

Wings: none
Body: peacock herl
Hackle: dark furnace
Tail: none

This is an old Welsh pattern whose name in that language means approximately "red and black". Initially tied as an imitation of the bracken clock (a small British beetle), the Coch-y-bondhu is undoubtedly the finest choice you can make when the manuka beetle is falling on the water around Christmas time here in New Zealand. The original pattern called for a Coch-y-bondhu hackle which is a dark reddish feather with black centre and black tips, but these are well-nigh impossible to obtain nowadays and a good dark furnace serves just as well. In addition, there also used to be a couple of turns of flat gold tinsel put on the shank before the body commenced, but it serves no purpose as far as I can determine, so I leave it off.

COACHMAN (D)

Wings: slips from any white primary wing feather
Body: peacock herl
Hackle: ginger

See Peveril of the Peak (page 137).

GREENWELL'S GLORY (D)

Wings: slips from blackbird or starling primary wing feathers
Body: primrose or light olive floss with fine gold tinsel spiralling up it
Hackle: originally coch-y-bondhu, nowadays a good dark furnace
Tail: none

A splendid pattern devised by the famous English Canon Greenwell about 150 years ago, this fly still works as well today as it did then even if, like me, you leave out the wings.

If I was ever forced to restrict myself to using only one pattern of dry fly this would probably be it. Indeed I *have* met several people in my fishing lifetime who had done just that, depending only on Greenwells tied in all sizes from 8 to 18 to cover every situation, and they seem to do as well as any of us!

HARDY'S FAVOURITE (D)

Wings: slips from hen pheasant primary wing feathers
Body: either red floss with peacock herl rib or peacock herl with red floss ribbing!
Hackle: speckled partridge
Tail: a few golden pheasant tippets

This is an extremely popular pattern in New

Zealand, but I have no idea why because I have yet to figure out how on earth you are supposed to get it to float, since the limp partridge hackle provides no support for the fly whatever! To overcome this I used to wind a good red cock hackle in along with the partridge, but of course the result then isn't really a Hardy's Favourite anymore and bears more of a resemblance to a Red-Tipped Governor (see page 138).

KAKAHI QUEEN (D)

Wings: slips from mallard primary wing feathers with slips of barred mallard feather dyed yellow tied alongside
Body: peacock herl quill with fibres removed
Hackle: usually furnace, but badger is used in some areas
Tail: bunch of hackle fibres from same type of feather as hackle

The Kakahi Queen is another all-New Zealand pattern which represents a wide variety of mayflies. Unfortunately, it is a tedious thing to tie in the traditional fashion, and my own version is considerably simpler:

Wings: none
Body: black floss with close ribbing of white thread running up it to produce black and white segmented effect
Hackle: dark badger
Tail: bunch of hackle fibres from same type of feather as hackle

MARCH BROWN (D)

Wings: slips from hen pheasant primary wing feathers
Body: roughly dubbed hare's fur, sometimes with an added ribbing of fine gold tinsel
Hackle: speckled brown partridge
Tail: partridge feather fibres

Although this traditional dressing makes an

excellent wet fly, dry flies so tied don't float well at all, since the limp webby partridge hackle provides no support whatever and the whole fly depends on the coarse hairs on the body for flotation. Personally when tying to order I add a good springy red or brown cock hackle, but for my own version I replace the partridge with a deep rich red hackle, use cock pheasant tail fibres for a tail and leave the wings off altogether, but I guess the result isn't really a March Brown then!

Another version called the Irish March Brown features a dubbed black seal's fur body and dyed claret hackle, and I've seen others with purple floss bodies and purple or black hackles which were alleged to be versions of the March Brown too.

PEVERIL OF THE PEAK (D)

Wings: white-tipped slips from blue part of a mallard's wing feathers
Body: peacock herl
Hackle: dark ginger, red or furnace
Tail: bunch of hackle fibres from same type of feather as hackle or sometimes a few golden pheasant tippets

Named after the hero in Sir Walter Scott's novel of the same name (God alone knows why, I've never been able to finish the book!), the Peveril is little more than a Coch-y-bondhu with a tail and wings, but the white tips on these wings really make it a lot easier to spot on rough water.

Tied with light ginger hackle and all-white wings, it becomes a Coachman, add a band of bright red floss in the mid-section of the Coachman and it becomes a Royal Coachman, or use a turn of red floss before starting the body and substitute hen pheasant feather for the wings, and you've got a Red-Tipped Governor near enough.

For my money, none of them will do anything a Coch-y-bondhu won't do except the white wings are a distinct advantage in conditions of failing light – or failing eyesight.

RED SPINNER (D)

Wings: slips from mallard, starling or blackbird primary wing feather
Body: bright red floss with fine gold tinsel spiralled up it
Hackle: reddish-ginger
Tail: bunch of fibres from same type of feather as hackle

A popular winged English dry fly which imitates nothing in particular as far as I can gather, but if you ever come across a mayfly with a bright red body let me know, and I'll retract that statement!

The name spinner is misleading, too. In entomological terms this is used to describe the last stages of a mayfly's life-cycle and in nature the insect has by then usually taken on a dull, drab appearance, totally unlike the bright, dashing, lively coloration of the Red Spinner. Nevertheless, it is an excellent and consistent taker of good trout.

RED-TIPPED GOVERNOR (D)

Wings: slips from hen pheasant primary wing feathers
Body: a couple of turns of bright red floss followed by a plump peacock herl body
Hackle: deep ginger
Tail: a small tag of red wool or floss

An excellent all-round New Zealand pattern, but frankly, like so many others, it's really only a winged derivation of the old Coch-y-bondhu.

ROYAL COACHMAN (D)

Wings: slips from any white primary wing feather
Body: peacock herl with a broad band of bright red floss in the middle
Hackle: ginger
Tail: golden pheasant tippets

Although representing nothing on earth, you'll find this gorgeous-looking fly in almost every dry-fly angler's box and, gaudy as it might appear, it catches plenty of fish. This fly is also sometimes tied with white hair wings, when it is known as a Royal Wulff, and Rotorua guide Geoff Thomas tells me he recommends it to his clientele as his single most productive dry-fly pattern. Considering guides *have* to get results or they don't stay in the business very long, this speaks for itself.

See also Peveril of the Peak (page 137).

TWILIGHT BEAUTY (D)

Wings: slips from mallard, blackbird or starling primary wing feathers
Body: black floss built up into a distinct bulge just behind hackle rather like the shape of a cupped ice-cream cone
Hackle: good bright ginger
Tail: bunch of fibres from same type of feather as hackle

Another good general all-round imitation covering many varieties of dark mayflies. Although I've listed several alternatives as wing materials, the older specimens I've seen of this very popular old New Zealand pattern all have really dark, almost inky-coloured wings, and to be honest I'm not exactly sure what feather they were tied from. However, any of the above will work just as well and, like so many other patterns, I don't bother putting wings on mine at all very often these days, with no apparent loss of effectiveness.

SALTWATER FLY FISHING

Many people are surprised to learn that you can take many species of marine fish on a fly using the same tackle you probably use at Taupo, but in America saltwater fly fishing is already big business.

There, the number of remaining quiet places in which the angler can cast a fly in the hope of catching a decent-sized fish in peace is shrinking rapidly as forests are hacked down, bush cleared and the land taken by "developers" (why don't they ever call them "exploiters"?) for new factories or industrial complexes and then for subdivisions in which to house the workforce. More land must be taken for the shops to serve them and yet more for carparks and adequate roading, then dams must be created to provide a supply of water, to produce extra electricity for lighting and power or for cooling systems in industry. As the watershed changes, even more dams have to be built and watercourses altered for irrigation and "improved" for flood control, until there are virtually no real natural undoctored rivers left in the area. In the State of California alone I understand there are only three sizable rivers left unruined (and this in an area bigger than all of New Zealand put together!), and even now plans are on hand for damming *them* up in order to pump their combined output the entire length of the state down to satisfy the insatiable demands of the ever-growing city of Los Angeles.

Of course, all these rivers and dams are labelled "recreational areas" and have nice little picnic tables and barbecues dotted around them, and the government makes up for the lack of natural trout-spawning facilities by dumping thousands of hatchery-reared fingerlings into the water each year, so in many places if you don't mind fishing for 20-cm trout among the water-skiers and the picnickers with their screaming kids, dogs, blaring transistor radios and litter, in still water with only a little industrial or urban pollution, that's OK; but if that isn't your scene you have a choice of pottering among the stagnant remains of a once-living river with picnickers and their screaming kids, dogs, blaring transistor radios and litter in the hope of rising a 15-cm trout before it dies from lack of oxygen or food.

Little wonder then that so many frustrated fly anglers have turned to the relative tranquillity of the bountiful ocean for their sport!

Here in New Zealand fortunately we haven't yet reached the level of exploitation of our heritage suffered by our American friends, but, God help us, we're working at it. I wonder how many of you realise that at the time of writing the government has plans for this "utilisation" of no less than twenty-seven of our rivers, some of which have *already* been destroyed. So don't think it can't happen here – it can and it *will* if politicians have their way and people remain apathetic. However, perhaps because there is still so much good trout fishing abundantly available in New Zealand, the need to seek and explore pastures new isn't so great, so saltwater fly fishing hasn't aroused the same interest here as it has overseas, but there is a growing awareness of its possibilities.

First of all, it's productive. My first trip to the ocean with my fly rod was in America about twenty years ago, and I came home with 38 lb (over 17 kg) of *fillets* – and that was my share after I divided the day's catch with two companions who'd come along just to watch! Here in New Zealand I've had absolutely fantastic sport, too, with kahawai, trevally, kingfish and barracouta, and sometimes such unlikely fish as snapper or maomao, and once even a John Dory.

Secondly, it's *fun*! I guarantee you'll be impressed the first time a kahawai seizes your fly and heads off for the great blue yonder — it makes a trout seem like an old boot in comparison.

Thirdly, there's no season, no limit and no licence required, and in addition you will frequently have an awful lot of ocean all to yourself.

Finally, if you're a world-record hunter there are few avenues where you'd have a better chance at getting your name in the book right now than in saltwater fly fishing. There is only one entry by a New Zealander there at present (January 1983) and that is a 14.5-kg (32-lb) southern yellowtail kingfish caught by my friend Dr Mike Godfrey of Mount Maunganui in 1979 on a 5-kg (12-lb) tippet, a tremendous effort involving a fight that lasted almost four hours incidentally! If catching a world record is your ambition, however, I recommend you ask your sports dealer for a copy of the I.G.F.A. rules since there are certain regulations involving tippet length, etc., which are critical.

Since saltwater flies usually represent some sort of small baitfish, you can get away with the same patterns you'd use for smelting trout — Grey Ghost, Jack Sprat, Silver Dorothy or Rabbit, for example — but you may like to try your hand at some more exotic patterns.

Here's one which I tie with the new synthetic FisHair. I guess it doesn't have to be as elaborate because I've found most hungry sea fish will grab anything moving which they can swallow, but it's easy to construct and fun to tie, so have a go.

HOW TO TIE A FISHAIR SALTWATER FLY

For this fly you'll need the following:

Mustad 34007 stainless steel hooks, size 1 or 2
Black FisHair
White FisHair
Yellow FisHair
Emerald-green FisHair
Peacock-blue FisHair
Wide silver Mylar
Monocord
Red head-cement
Clear body-cement

1. Bind hook shank with thread and tie in wide silver Mylar. Take a pinch of white FisHair (about $\frac{1}{3}$ of what you think you'll need!) and tie in so tail extends about same length as hook shank and butt ends about $\frac{1}{2}$ way up shank. Give this body section a light touch of clear body-cement.

Fig 40

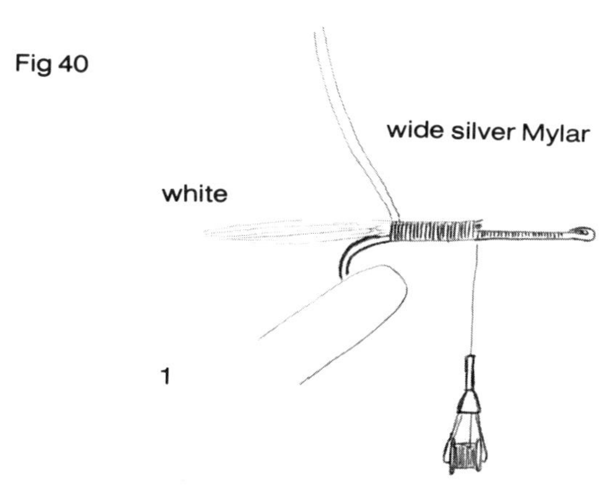

2. Bind over with Mylar in overlapping wraps and tie in when you reach the end of the white butt, but don't cut it off. Take another pinch of FisHair, yellow this time, and tie in with the butts being bound up to $\frac{3}{4}$ way along shank. Lightly coat with clear cement.

Fig 40 continued

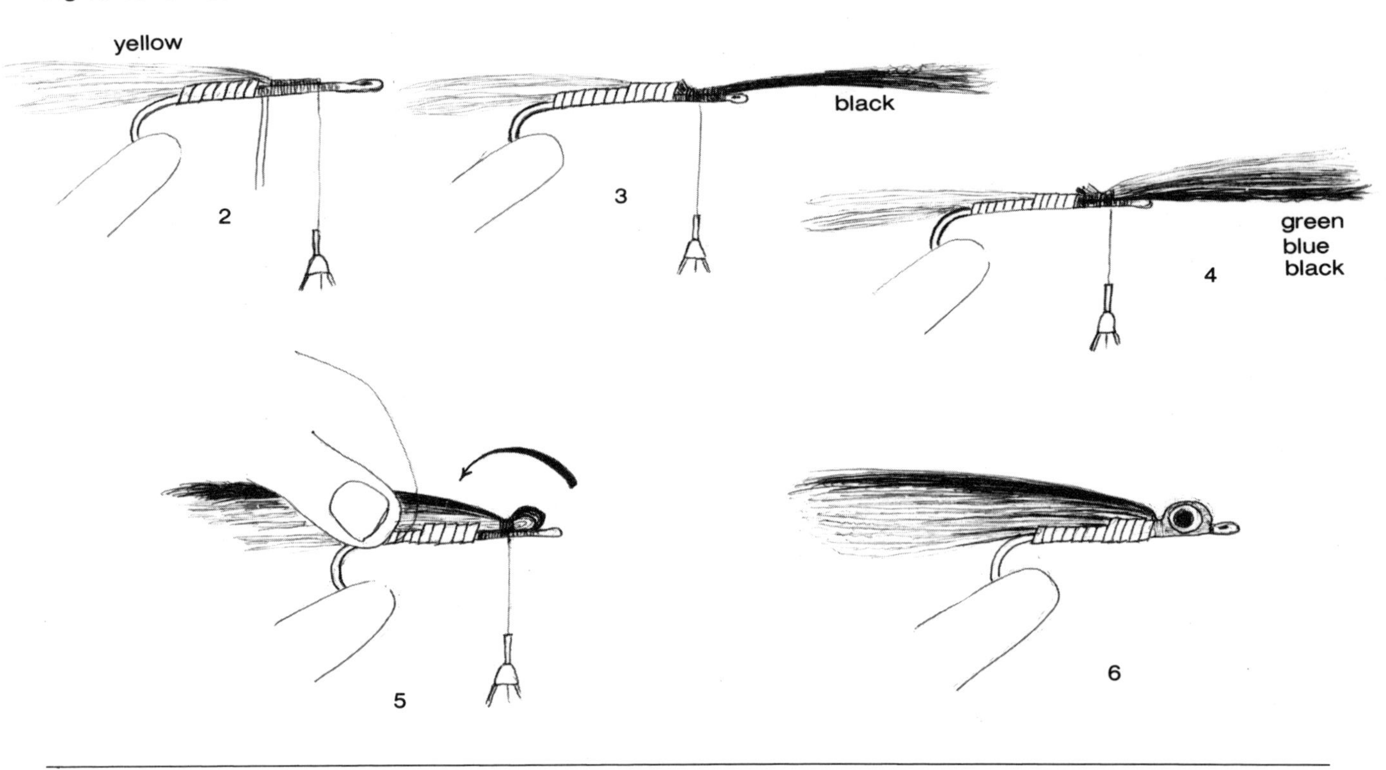

3. Continue overlapping with Mylar to the end of the yellow, tie in and trim surplus. Lay a wisp of black FisHair pointing *forwards* with butts up against butts of yellow and secure with 3 or 4 turns of thread.
4. Repeat with a wisp of peacock-blue, then again with emerald-green on top.
5. Now grip all these and fold back over the body. Hold there while you wind half a dozen turns of thread around the "neck", then bring thread to behind the eye of the hook and whip-finish and cut free.
6. Saturate the "head" (i.e. from the whip-finish back to the "neck") with clear cement. When dry, recoat with red cement.

Although totally unnecessary, a very pleasing effect can be obtained by the addition of "eyes". Get a tiny tin of white enamel from a hobby shop (it's used for painting model aeroplanes and the like), and with the finest artist's brush you can locate, apply a spot of white to each side of the head. When dry, add little pupils of black head-cement. The finished result you'll find has really "come to life", but eyes on flies have another use besides aesthetics, as I discovered some years back. I have a friend who just never seemed to have the right fly in his king-size fly box, and on fishing trips he was forever borrowing from me. I was more than happy to oblige, but at the end of the day he'd say, "Here's your fly back" and hand me the last one he'd borrowed. When I'd ask about the others, he'd look all hurt and say, "Why I gave them back as I changed flies, but you can look for yourself if you like", and hand me his fly box. One day I'd just finished "eyeing" a batch of saltwater flies and, on impulse, took out my boxes of lake lures and added eyes to all the inhabitants while I had the white enamel and brush handy. This was no mean task, for they totalled 20 or 30 dozen as I recall, but it was a bad day and I hadn't much else to do anyway.

Next time we went fishing and I was offered the opportunity to check my friend's fly box for "kidnapped victims" I said, "Oh, they'd be easy to spot, mine are all eyed", and I watched his face redden as he opened his box and saw all the little eyes staring back at him in mute testimony!

Incidentally, stainless steel hooks are notoriously blunt even when brand-new, so it's a good idea to hone the points needle sharp before use. Fig. 41 shows the shape and sizes available.

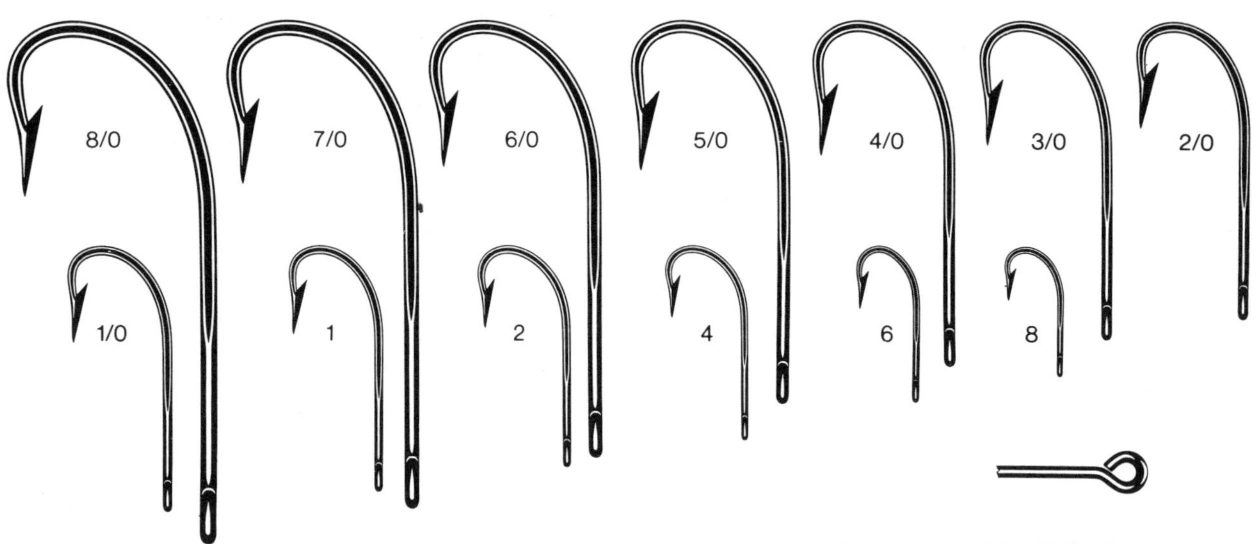

Fig 41 Mustad 34007 for Saltwater hooks

NEW MATERIALS

In their endless quest for the ultimate, lifelike artificial fly, fly tyers the world over are constantly searching for new and better materials with which to tie it, and if they can't find what they are looking for some of them, particularly our American friends, actually develop it themselves.

Here are just a few examples of some of the more recent ones.

FISHAIR

This is a synthetic hair which has virtually replaced bucktail as a material for tying many flies and streamers. Available in red, fluorescent orange, tangerine, yellow, peacock-blue, silver-blue, white, squirrel-brown and black, the last two colours being very useful substitutes for black and brown squirrel tail. Each colour comes as a swatch of fibres heat-sealed together at one end, all the shades are colour-fast so the dyes won't run when wet, and it appears to be fade-proof and moth-proof as well. Two sizes are currently marketed, *large* for making saltwater game-fishing lures and *small* for fly tying.

There is an illustrated guide to tying a saltwater streamer fly using FisHair on page 143–5.

POLYCRYOLIN YARN

An amazing material which surprisingly doesn't enjoy nearly as much popularity as it deserves, Polycryolin is actually three things in one:

(a) Used as shown in fig. 42 it makes superb dubbed bodies for wets, dries and nymphs.

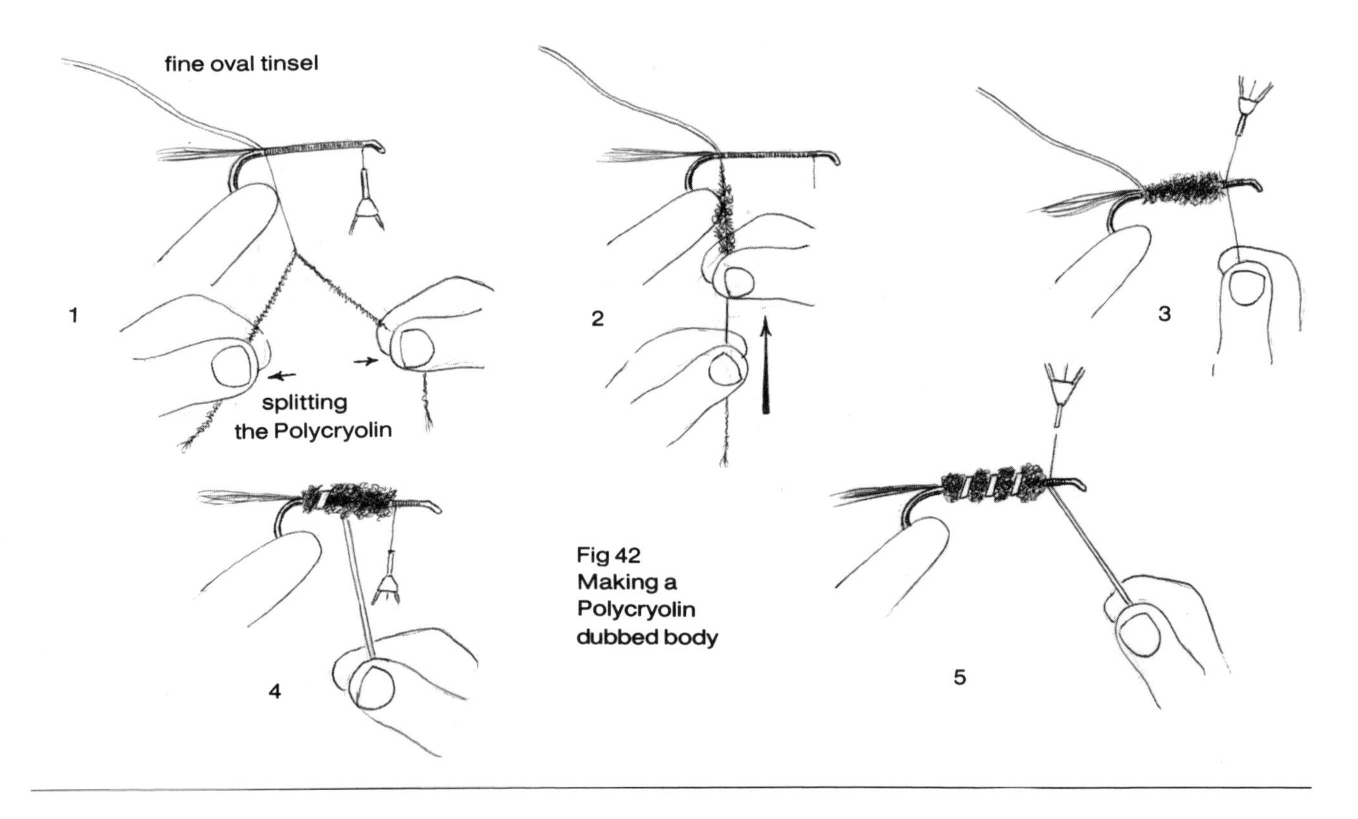

Fig 42
Making a
Polycryolin
dubbed body

(b) Wound tightly it can be used in lieu of floss as a body material.
(c) Used even more tightly it doubles as a fly-tying thread where something stronger than Monocord is required.

This comes in 12 different colours and is sold in individual spools or in a handy transparent dispenser holding all of them. Slots in the sides allow material to be pulled out as required without having to remove the lid.

HOW TO MAKE A POLYCRYOLIN DUBBED BODY

1. Tie in a piece of Polycryolin perhaps 8 cm long after you've done the tail and tied in a length of fine oval tinsel. Wind the thread up to where the body will end. Split the Polycryolin in two.
2. Holding the left strand tightly stretched, push the right one up it toward the hook shank, thus forming a sort of dubbed-fur effect along the left strand.
3. Wind this "dubbed" strand up the shank to form a body, tie down with thread and trim surplus.

4-5. Because it tends to be very fluffy and unruly I like to add additional security by using a rib of fine oval tinsel spiralled up over the length of the body. This also creates a sort of segmented appearance similar to the bodies of many natural aquatic creatures, but you could, as an alternative, use another piece of Polycryolin or thread (in lieu of the tinsel) in either a matching or contrasting colour.

FLASHABOU

For centuries it has been known that the flashing sides of darting baitfish are a key factor in stimulating the killer instincts of many predatory gamefish. Accordingly, fly-tyers over the years have traditionally used tinsel bodies on many of their baitfish imitations in an attempt to duplicate this flash.

Recently, however, the Americans have come

up with a new material which may well eventually replace tinsel for this purpose. Called "Flashabou", it consists of fine strands of super-limp, super-reflective mylar, a couple of which tied in at each side of the head and allowed to drape down the sides of any pattern will add such glitter and "life" when the fly is retrieved through the water, you have see it to believe it!

Try adding a few strands of gold to your next "Parsons Glory" or silver to a "Jack Spratt" or perhaps pearl to a "Grey Ghost", and you'll see what I mean (see Fig 43). But don't overdo it: as with so many things, a little goes a long way.

With saltwater patterns, however, you can make an exception. Here it's a case of "the more the merrier", and you can tie Flashabou in bunches in much the same way as you would "Fishair". All colours seem to work, but combinations of blue over green over silver have proved particularly good for me.

Fig 43 Using Flashabou

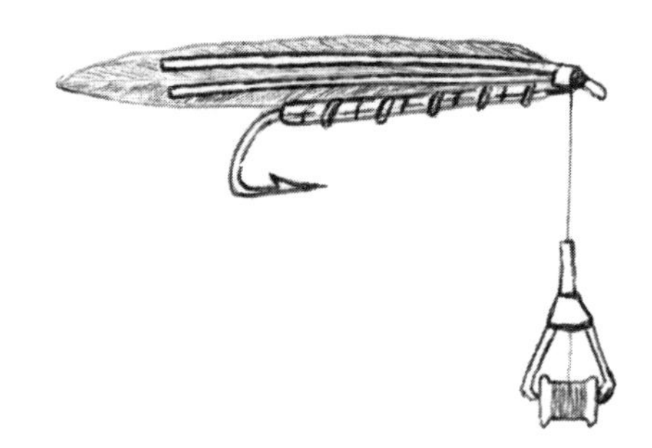

SWANNUNDAZE

A thin plastic ribbon-like material which can be used to create the most realistic segmented nymph bodies imaginable, Swannundaze comes in two widths, $\frac{3}{32}$ in and $\frac{1}{32}$ in, and a wide variety of colours from black to cream, many of which are translucent. A strand or two of one of the darker shades makes an excellent alternative material for wing-cases and, bound over a pale floss underbody, the translucent versions really "glow" like a fat, juicy natural. Transparent Swannundaze can be bound over silver-bodied flies to give a natural scalelike appearance as well as provide added protection from teeth (particularly useful in saltwater patterns), and I recently saw some interesting silver rabbits where the tyer had not only bound the Mylar body with a protective overwrap of fine transparent Swannundaze, but had used a spiral of it to hold the strip of rabbit pelt fast to the top of the shank in lieu of the traditional oval tinsel.

Here are two tips to remember when using Swannundaze:

1. Before tying in, cut the end to be initially secured in a long, tapering angle. This will avoid an ugly bulge building up as you start to wind up the shank.
2. Swannundaze stretches and becomes much more supple when warm, so generate some frictional heat by drawing it quickly between finger and thumb a few times before making a body. The material will then form lovely snug segments while warm, shrinking into a really tightly locked shape when it cools off a minute or two later.

RANDOM THOUGHTS ON AQUATIC VERMIN

Having learned to tie our first flies, we are all anxious to try them out at the earliest opportunity and so, although not *directly* connected with fly tying, I'd like to use this space to say a few words about fishing behaviour.

An American once said there are three things that people hate most – cold coffee, wet toilet paper and a smartass! While I agree, I can think of three others which I detest just as much.

THE LITTER LOUT

These despicable creatures, like the poor, are always with us and unfortunately appear to be on the increase. You can trace their footsteps by following the trail of empty cigarette cartons, bits of cellophane and candy wrappers and see where they fed by the mess of empty bottles, cans, orange peel and banana skins, while the sites of lure and leader changes are marked by bits of plastic, empty spools and lengths of tangled nylon. You'll probably find the newspaper from their fish and chip suppers blowing along the roadside on the way home, too. I can remember narrowly averting death on my motorcycle when my head was totally enveloped in such a wrapper flung from a speeding car ahead of me.

What selfish, thoughtless, inconsiderate pests these people are! Have they never seen the dreadful wounds broken bottles or rusty cans are capable of inflicting? My friend Peter had his pedigree bitch ruined for show purposes when she had a playful roll in the grass where a jagged piece of broken beer bottle lay hidden and rose yelping and bleeding minus a sizable chunk of her ear.

Have they never considered the number of wild birds which pick up waste nylon for nesting material and carry it into the bush only to become hopelessly entangled in the stuff? A long, lingering death by strangulation or starvation follows as they hang there suspended and helpless, unable to escape from the clutches of the near-invisible killer material? I have seen the grisly remains many times, and it's not a pretty sight. Neither is the sight of cattle's tongues almost severed clean through at the roots by the frightening cutting power of waste nylon they've inadvertently tried to chew, or the hideous damage done to their legs when they become entangled in nylon.

I nearly lost my own life once when I'd waded out into a strong, deep current to cast to a rising fish unreachable from the bank and found my feet almost totally hobbled by a tangled mess of monofilament caught up in an underwater snag. The current was too strong and too deep for me to reach down and cut myself free, and there was no one in sight to call upon for help. Since I wasn't expected back at camp until after dark, it was unlikely anyone would come looking for me until very much later, and the area wasn't one where I'd expect to see many other anglers. Hard as I tried, I could not move either of my feet more than a few inches backward or forward, and I felt the first wave of panic as I considered how easy it would be to drown if I tried too hard and overbalanced. I had just made the decision to jettison my bulky vest, cut the waders free from my legs as best I could and swim for it, when mercifully the snag broke away from its parent trunk and I was able to slowly shuffle my way back to safety, where I sat shakily smoking a cigarette and wishing I could have got my hands on the slob who'd dumped the lethal coils in the river to begin with.

Some years ago a vet showed me a collection of things he'd removed from cattle stomachs over his 20 years of practice. It included such unlikely things as golf balls, golf tees, handkerchiefs, a cloth cap, empty shotgun shells, cigarette packets, matchboxes and matchbooks, a huge piece of plastic sheeting about two metres square and several plastic monofilament spools, as well as vast quantities of nylon monofilament itself.

So the moral of all this is, please don't litter! Aside from being unsightly, it can be dangerous to both domestic animals and wildlife as well as humans, as you have learned, and even the ubiquitous banana skin or orange peel, biodegradable or not, has caused many a nasty fall by the riverside as well as on the city streets. So if you take it there, take it back with you!

THE FISH HOG

Members of this selfish, greedy breed often aren't as easy to spot right off, but will always give themselves away after a few moments of conversation or a short period of fishing with them. They apparently suffer from a dreadful inferiority complex which compels them to bolster their dwindling egos by killing as many fish as possible and then bragging about their "success" to anyone who wants to listen and frequently those who don't. Often accomplished and experienced anglers, they will accompany you to a favourite "secret" fishing spot only you knew about, then having learned its location, regularly return alone or with fellow hogs, killing everything they catch until the area is fished out. Perhaps through jealousy they will decry the activities of poachers, but before they have finished their drink they will be bragging about how they caught way over the limit and managed to avoid the ranger. The only fish they return are those that can't be stretched to the 14 in (35 cm) limit size when they suspect someone of authority may be watching, but unfortunately few trout survive this ordeal anyway. Borderline cases are killed on the grounds that "the small fish taste the sweetest".

Many fish hogs are so greedy they would no more think of going fishing without their smoking, canning and bottling plant than they would without their fishing rods, frequently taking away so much smoked, bottled and canned trout that they cannot use it or even give it away to friends, so are forced to try to sell it or raffle it off in the pub.

You'll often find they have beautiful gardens. I saw why when I saw one burying 11 big trout among his roses — he'd had to take them out of his deep freeze to make room for the previous day's catch, he said, adding that since they'd been there 12 months they were probably suffering from freezer burn anway. What a diabolical waste of prime game fish. So don't become a fish hog! Limit your kill to what you can use instead of killing your limit just to prove how good you are. Nobody really cares that much anyway.

THE IGNORANT PIG

This is the one who arrives at the river as you are tackling up, rushes past you to the first pool so as to fish it first, but after a few unproductive casts splashes across it and scrambles up the bank (scaring the pants off any fish in the immediate vicinity in the process) to rush into the next pool before you get there too, and he's the one who will blithely stride into the river ahead of a line of anglers waiting their turns to fish an occupied reach.

I remember a ferret-faced little creature who regularly committed this infuriating and selfish act on the Tongariro. Muttering "You don't mind if I go in ahead, do you?", he'd go in anyway, apparently unaware of the not always complimentary comments regarding his parentage from the other anglers. One day I was fishing down the Major Jones pool behind an enormous Hawkes Bay sheep cocky when this little pest scuttled out of the lupins and into the water ahead of the big man. "OY!" he yelled, "What the HELL do you think you're doing?" Ferret-face glanced back over his shoulder. "Oh, I'm in a bit of a hurry. You don't mind, do you?" "Too bloody right I do!" came the reply, and then in a voice that I'll bet his dogs responded to back in Hawkes Bay, "GET IN BEHIND!"

I've never seen anyone move so fast as that little pig did, stumbling ashore in a flurry of foam and disappearing among the lupins while still winding line back onto his reel. After he'd gone the big man turned to me, and winding in his own line he said, "I'm sorry about that, but that little b——d has been doing that to me all week, and I thought it was time somebody taught him a lesson. I tell you if he *hadn't* moved, I'd have broken his bloody neck! Now I feel all upset and it's spoiled my fishing, so I'm off! You can have the pool to yourself."

I'm sorry my farmer friend had his fishing ruined, but if he ever reads this he may gain some satisfaction in learning that his treatment worked, for I've never seen ferret-face on the river again to this day.

Some ignorant pigs are ardent boaties, and they will often race you to the launch ramp and then park there for 20 minutes holding everyone up while they load the boat and prepare it for launching, instead of doing all that *before* backing to the ramp. Once afloat they must show just how fast they can go off through the moorings, often sending meals sliding onto the laps of irate diners in other boats moored nearby, slopping water over the tops of anglers' waders and occasionally swamping small dinghies.

You'll spot them again when you're anchored at the Delta quietly fishing the rip. One will anchor up alongside to starboard and let out the mooring line until his boat has effectively blocked any casting you were doing, which won't really matter because once *he* starts casting you'll be afraid of raising your head above the gunwales lest you lose an eye!

Or perhaps at sea you've just located a shoal of feeding kahawai and are working your fly along the edge of the mob, when the ignorant pig will arrive and steam right through the middle of them trolling a huge lure more suited to bluefin tuna than a kahawai. The shoal will scatter and sound, and you'll have to wait for them to reappear, but you're wasting your time because so will ignorant pig, and the instant they show, he'll be right through the middle of them to repeat the performance.

Camping is another favourite pursuit of this species, and I'll bet you've come across a few of them in your time. They're the ones who burn all the firewood you collected earlier in the day so you wouldn't have to go searching for more when you got back from fishing after dark, or keep their radios at full blast half the night when you have an early start planned for the morning and need a good night's sleep. They're also the ones who leave their cars parked in the middle of the only firm access road to your intended campsite, which necessitates your having several-hundred-metre walks to and from your car to set up the camp or else facing a hazardous detour through some dangerous-looking swampy ground.

They will bring their litters down to the river and tell them it's all right to play there so long as they don't annoy the man fishing, and they will go swimming and shrieking out of control all over the place totally ruining your fishing while the sows recline in the shade listening to the racing results and the "top half million" pops, their wretched transistors full-bore, until in despair you are forced to up-camp and try to find peace and solitude elsewhere.

But I'm not telling you anything you don't know already. Just remember to give others some courtesy, ask permission before you to on to private property, and be careful with gates, fences, crops, livestock and where you park — like not across the only entrance to the river flats paddock. Farmers have feelings, too, you know! Be considerate to other campers and anglers, and always offer a helping hand, especially to "new chums": we all have to learn some time. If you must have a fire, keep it small and under control, and make sure it's thoroughly extinguished before leaving it. All rubbish should be burned or buried; better still, take it away with you. And don't kill any more fish than you can use.Fish can usually be carefully returned to live and fight another day.

CONCLUSION

Well, by now you should have grasped the fundamentals of fly tying, and although your first attempts may be crude, with a little practice it won't be long before you are turning out flies that are just as good as (or probably better than) those you used to buy from the shop. After all, you're not being forced to produce so many per hour in order to make a living, and therefore you've got the time to ensure every stage is perfect before going on to the next one, to make sure hackles, tails and wings are lying exactly the way they should be, to triple whip-finish heads and carefully apply the cement without clogging the eyes of the hooks. So be patient, take your time and practise often. Soon most things you've had difficulty in mastering will become almost automatic, and you'll wonder what the problem ever was to begin with. Eventually you'll find yourself teaching others what you've learned and you'll find, as I so often have, the added enjoyment of watching the delight on the novice's face as he or she finishes their very first fly. You'll meet others whose fly-tying ability is greater or less than yours, too, and there is a lot of satisfaction to be obtained in learning from the former and in passing on your knowledge to the latter.

There are more ways than one of killing the cat, as the old adage tells us, and this also applies to many aspects of fly tying for, as you progress, you will indeed find there are often several alternative methods of producing the same result or effect.

The methods I've described are the ones which, from experience, work best or have become most comfortable for me, but if you come across a different approach to a given problem, by all means give it a try. It may very well suit you better than mine.

There are literally thousands of standard fly patterns in existence today, not to mention the myriads of variations and local adaptations of them. To describe all of them would entail years of work and result in a volume several times the size and cost of this one. Neither have I gone into the intricacies of how to tie "parachute flies", double split-wing, no-hackle flies or detached body mayflies, to name but a few alternative specialties. As I have stressed earlier, this was never intended to be either a dictionary of flies or a complete encyclopaedia of fly tying. What I wanted to do was to produce a book which everyone could afford and which illustrated clearly and simply how to tie basic artificial flies, primarily to assist those who have never done it before, but also as a guide to overseas tyers who are not familiar with the design and construction techniques used in the unique big New Zealand flies. I have tried to make everything clear and easy to understand, and if this book enables you to derive half the enjoyment from tying your own flies (and catching fish with them!) as I have with mine over my lifetime, both of us will be very happy.

Tight lines!

Hugh McDowell
Ngongotaha 1983

INDEX OF FLY PATTERNS

H = Hackle-style fly
M = Matuku-style fly
P = Pukeko-style fly
K = Killer-style fly
O = Big lure not in above categories
N = Nymph
W = Wet fly
D = Dry fly

1 2 3

Tail
+ Tag.

Possum / Rabbit
Dyed.

Burglar

George Garchell.
Taupo Turangi.

Sinking / Still water.